Talent Is Overrated

Talent Is Overrated

What *Really* Separates World-Class Performers from Everybody Else

GEOFF COLVIN   *Portfolio*

PORTFOLIO

Published by the Penguin Group

Penguin Group (USA) Inc., 375 Hudson Street, New York, New York 10014, U.S.A. · Penguin Group (Canada), 90 Eglinton Avenue East, Suite 700, Toronto, Ontario, Canada M4P 2Y3 (a division of Pearson Penguin Canada Inc.) · Penguin Books Ltd, 80 Strand, London WC2R 0RL, England · Penguin Ireland, 25 St. Stephen's Green, Dublin 2, Ireland (a division of Penguin Books Ltd) · Penguin Books Australia Ltd, 250 Camberwell Road, Camberwell, Victoria 3124, Australia (a division of Pearson Australia Group Pty Ltd) · Penguin Books India Pvt Ltd, 11 Community Centre, Panchsheel Park, New Delhi–110 017, India · Penguin Group (NZ), 67 Apollo Drive, Rosedale, North Shore 0632, New Zealand (a division of Pearson New Zealand Ltd) · Penguin Books (South Africa) (Pty) Ltd, 24 Sturdee Avenue, Rosebank, Johannesburg 2196, South Africa

Penguin Books Ltd, Registered Offices: 80 Strand, London WC2R 0RL, England

First published in 2008 by Portfolio, a member of Penguin Group (USA) Inc.

10   9   8   7

LIBRARY OF CONGRESS CATALOGING-IN-PUBLICATION DATA

Colvin, Geoffrey.

   Talent is overrated : what *really* separates world-class performers from everybody else / by Geoff Colvin.

      p.   cm.

Includes bibliographical references and index.

ISBN 978-1-59184-224-8

1. Work—Psychological aspects.   2. Performance.   I. Title.

BF481.C625 2008

153.9—dc22   2008024976

Printed in the United States of America

Designed by Carla Bolte · Set in Celeste

For my sons

Contents

Talent Is Overrated

The Mystery

Great performance is more valuable than ever—
but where does it really come from?

It is mid-1978, and we are inside the giant Procter & Gamble head-quarters in Cincinnati, looking into a cubicle shared by a pair of twenty-two-year-old men, fresh out of college. Their assignment is to help sell Duncan Hines brownie mix, but they spend a lot of their time just re-writing memos according to strict company rules. They are clearly smart: one has just graduated from Harvard, the other from Dartmouth. But that doesn't distinguish them from a slew of other new hires at P&G. What does distinguish them from many of the young go-getters the company takes on each year is that neither man is particularly filled with ambition. Neither has any kind of career plan or any specific ca-reer goals. Every afternoon they play waste-bin basketball with wadded-up memos. One of them later recalls, "We were voted the two guys probably least likely to succeed."

These two young men are of interest to us now for only one reason: They are Jeffrey Immelt and Steven Ballmer, who before age fifty would become CEOs of the world's two most valuable corporations, General Electric and Microsoft. Contrary to what any reasonable person would have expected when they were new recruits, they reached the absolute apex of corporate achievement. The obvious question is how.

Was it talent? If so, it was a strange kind of talent that hadn't revealed itself in the first twenty-two years of their lives. Was it brains? These two were sharp but had shown no evidence of being sharper than thousands of their classmates or colleagues. Was it mountains of hard work? Certainly not up to that point.

And yet something carried them to the heights of the business world. Which leads to perhaps the most puzzling question, one that applies not just to Immelt and Ballmer but also to everyone in our lives and to ourselves: If that certain something turns out not to be any of the the things we usually think of, then what is it?

Look around you.

Look at your friends, your relatives, your coworkers, the people you meet when you shop or go to a party. How do they spend their days? Most of them work. They all do many other things as well, playing sports, performing music, pursuing hobbies, doing public service. Now ask yourself honestly: How well do they do what they do?

The most likely answer is that they do it fine. They do it well enough to keep doing it. At work they don't get fired and probably get promoted a number of times. They play sports or pursue their other interests well enough to enjoy them. But the odds are that few if any of the people around you are truly great at what they do—awesomely, amazingly, world-class excellent.

Why—exactly why—aren't they? Why don't they manage businesses like Jack Welch or Andy Grove, or play golf like Tiger Woods, or play the violin like Itzhak Perlman? After all, most of them are good, conscientious people, and they probably work diligently. Some of them have been at it for a very long time—twenty, thirty, forty years. Why isn't that enough to make them great performers? It clearly isn't. The hard truth is that virtually none of them has achieved greatness or come even close, and only a tiny few ever will.

This is a mystery so commonplace that we scarcely notice it, yet it's critically important to the success or failure of our organizations, the causes we believe in, and our own lives. In some cases we can give plausible explanations, saying that we're less than terrific at hobbies and games because we don't take them all that seriously. But what about our work? We prepare for it through years of education and devote most of our waking hours to it. Most of us would be embarrassed to add up the total hours we've spent on our jobs and then compare that number with the hours we've given to other priorities that we claim are more important, like our families; the figures would show that work is our real priority. Yet after all those hours and all those years, most people are just okay at what they do.

In fact the reality is more puzzling than that. Extensive research in a wide range of fields shows that many people not only fail to become outstandingly good at what they do, no matter how many years they spend doing it, they frequently don't even get any better than they were when they started. Auditors with years of experience were no better at detecting corporate fraud—a fairly important skill for an auditor—than were freshly trained rookies. When it comes to judging personality disorders, which is one of the things we count on clinical psychologists to do, length of clinical experience told nothing about skill—"the correlations," concluded some of the leading researchers, "are roughly zero." Surgeons were no better at predicting hospital stays after surgery than residents were. In field after field, when it came to centrally important skills—stockbrokers recommending stocks, parole officers predicting recidivism, college admissions officials judging applicants—people with lots of experience were no better at their jobs than those with very little experience.

The most recent studies of business managers confirm these results. Researchers from the INSEAD business school in France and the U.S. Naval Postgraduate School call the phenomenon "the experience trap." Their key finding: While companies typically value experienced managers, rigorous study shows that, on average, "managers with experience did not produce high-caliber outcomes."

Bizarre as this seems, in at least a few fields it gets one degree odder. Occasionally people actually get worse with experience. More experienced doctors reliably score lower on tests of medical knowledge than do less experienced doctors; general physicians also become less skilled over time at diagnosing heart sounds and X-rays. Auditors become less skilled at certain types of evaluations.

What is especially troubling about these findings is the way they deepen, rather than solve, the mystery of great performance. When asked to explain why a few people are so excellent at what they do, most of us have two answers, and the first one is hard work. People get extremely good at something because they work hard at it. We tell our kids that if they just work hard, they'll be fine. It turns out that this is exactly right. They'll be fine, just like all those other people who work at something for most of their lives and get along perfectly acceptably but never become particularly good at it. The research confirms that merely putting in the years isn't much help to someone who wants to be a great performer.

So our instinctive first answer to the question of exceptional performance does not hold up.

Our second answer is the opposite of the first, but that doesn't stop us from believing it fervently. It goes back at least twenty-six hundred years, to the time of Homer:

> Call in the inspired bard
> Demodocus. God has given the man the gift of song.

That's from the *Odyssey,* one of many references in it and the *Iliad* to the god-given gifts of various characters. We've changed our views on a lot of important matters since then— how the planets move, where diseases come from—but we have not changed our views on what makes some people extraordinarily good at what they do. We still think what Homer thought: that the awesomely great, apparently superhuman performers around us came into this world with a gift for doing exactly what they ended up doing—in the case of Demodocus, composing and singing. We use the same words that the ancient Greeks used, simply translated. We still say, as Homer did, that great performers are inspired, meaning that their greatness was breathed into them by gods or muses. We still say they have a gift, which is to say their greatness was given to them, for reasons no one can explain, by someone or something apart from themselves.

We believe further that such people had the great good fortune to discover their gift, usually early in life. While this explanation of great performance obviously contradicts the just-work-hard explanation, it's much more deeply rooted and in some ways is more satisfying. It explains why great performers seem to do effortlessly certain things that most of us can't imagine doing at all, whether it's forming a strategy for a multibillion-dollar company or playing the Tchaikovsky Violin Concerto or hitting a golf ball 330 yards. The natural-gift explanation also explains why extraordinary performers are so rare; god-given talents are presumably not handed out willy-nilly.

This explanation has the additional advantage of helping most of us come to somewhat melancholy terms with our own performance. A god-given gift is a one-in-a-million thing. You have it or you don't. If you don't—and of course most of us don't—then it follows that you should just forget now about ever coming close to greatness.

Thus it's clear why most of us don't dwell on the mystery of great performance. We don't think it's a mystery. We've got a couple of explanations in our head, and if it ever occurs to us that the first one is clearly wrong, well, the second one is what we really believe anyway. And the nicest thing about the second explanation is that it takes the matter of great performance out of our hands. If we were really a natural at anything, we'd know it by now. Since we're not, we can worry about other things.

The trouble with this explanation—except it isn't trouble, it's excellent news—is that it's wrong. Great performance is in our hands far more than most of us ever suspected.

New Findings on Great Performance

It turns out that our knowledge of great performance, like our knowledge of everything else, has actually advanced quite a bit in the past couple of millennia. It's just that most of the findings haven't made their way into people's heads. Scientists began turning their attention to it in a big way about 150 years ago, but what's most important is the growing mountain of research that has accumulated in just the past 30 years. Conducted by scientists around the world, who have looked into top-level performance in a wide array of fields, including management, chess, swimming, surgery, jet piloting, violin playing, sales, novel writing, and many others, these hundreds of research studies have converged on some major conclusions that directly contradict most of what we all think we know about great performance. Specifically:

• The gifts possessed by the best performers are not at all what we think they are. They are certainly not enough to explain the achievements of such people—and that's if these gifts exist at all. Some researchers now argue that specifically targeted innate abilities are simply fiction. That is, you are not a natural-born clarinet virtuoso or car salesman or bond trader or brain surgeon—because no one is. Not all researchers are prepared to accept that view, but the talent advocates have a surprisingly difficult time demonstrating that even those natural gifts they believe they can substantiate are particularly important in attaining great performance.

• Going beyond the question of specific innate gifts, even the general abilities that we typically believe characterize the greats are not what we think. In many realms—chess, music, business, medicine—we assume that the outstanding performers must possess staggering intelligence or gigantic memories. Some do, but many do not. For example, some people have become international chess masters though they possess below-average IQs. So whatever it is that makes these people special, it doesn't depend on superhuman general abilities. On that score, a great many of them are amazingly average.

• The factor that seems to explain the most about great performance is something the researchers call deliberate practice. Exactly what that is and isn't turns out to be extremely important. It definitely isn't what most of us do on the job every day, which begins to explain the great mystery of the workplace—why we're surrounded by so many people who have worked hard for decades but have never approached greatness. Deliberate practice is also not what most of us do when we think we're practicing golf or the oboe or any of our other interests. Deliberate practice is hard. It hurts. But it works. More of it equals better performance. Tons of it equals great performance.

While there's a lot to be said about deliberate practice, a few initial observations are key:

• Deliberate practice is a large concept, and to say that it explains everything would be simplistic and reductive. Critical questions immediately present themselves: What exactly needs to be practiced? Precisely how? Which specific skills or other assets must be acquired? The research has revealed answers that generalize quite well across a wide range of fields. It certainly seems daunting to seek a common explanation for greatness in ballet and medical diagnosis, or insurance sales and baseball, but a few key factors do seem to account for top performance in those realms and many more.

• Most organizations are terrible at applying the principles of great performance. Many companies seem arranged almost perfectly to prevent people from taking advantage of these principles for themselves or for the teams in which they work. That situation presents a great opportunity for companies that understand the principles and apply them widely.

• One of the most important questions about greatness surrounds the difficulty of deliberate practice. The chief constraint is mental, regardless of the field—even in sports, where we might think the physical demands are the hardest. Across realms, the required concentration is so intense that it's exhausting. If deliberate practice is so hard—if in most cases it's "not inherently enjoyable," as some of the top researchers say—then why do some people put themselves through it day after day for decades, while most do not? Where does the necessary passion come from? That turns out to be quite a deep question. But answers are turning up.

The new understanding of great performance is especially powerful because it seems widely generalizable. Researchers continue to test it in an increasingly broad range of fields, and it keeps holding up. So the opportunity to apply it in all types of domains seems irresistible, and indeed doing so looks increasingly like an urgent task.

You might say that this new understanding has come along just in the nick of time, because the need for it in every field is greater than ever. The reasons are many. Most apparent is the trend of rapidly rising standards in virtually every domain. To overstate only slightly, people everywhere are doing and making pretty much everything better. We see examples wherever we turn, starting in our own households. You're well aware that computers offer more power for fewer dollars every year, but the same phenomenon is happening across industries. How long did your parents' car last? Maybe 50,000 miles? If you put 200,000 miles on your new Toyota, no one will think anything of it. It's a similar story with the car's tires. A Whirlpool washer (or any other major brand) has more functions, uses less water, requires less electricity, and costs far less in inflation-adjusted dollars than it did five years ago. In every industry worldwide, businesses have to perform at the highest standard, and then get continually better, just to be competitive. Great performance is becoming more valuable.

The trend is the same in virtually every field of individual human performance. Consider sports, which not only are interesting in themselves but also, as we shall see, have much to teach us about great performance in business and other realms—and not in the old-fashioned winning-is-the-only-thing sense. We all know that sports records keep getting broken, but we generally don't appreciate just how dramatic the progress has been, or the reasons for it. For example, the Olympic records of a hundred years ago—representing the best performance of any human being on the planet—today in many cases equal ho-hum performance by high schoolers. The winner of the men's 200-meter race in the 1908 Olympics ran it in 22.6 seconds; today's high school record is faster by more than 2 seconds, a huge margin. Today's best high school time in the marathon beats the 1908 Olympic gold medalist by more than twenty minutes. And if you're thinking it's because kids today are bigger, that's not it. Recent research by Dr. Niels H. Secher of the University of Copenhagen and others shows that size is no advantage in running, since each stride requires you to lift yourself up. "The smaller you are, the better you are," he says.

In any case, events in which size and power are irrelevant show the same pattern of constantly rising standards. In diving, for example, the double somersault was almost prohibited as recently as the 1924 Olympics because it was considered too dangerous. Today, it's boring.

This matters because of why it's happening: Contemporary athletes are superior not because they're somehow different but because they train themselves more effectively. That's an important concept for us to remember.

Standards in intellectual disciplines are rising at least as fast as in sports. Roger Bacon, the great English scholar and teacher of the thirteenth century, wrote that a person would need thirty to forty years of study to master mathematics as then understood. Today the math he was talking about—calculus hadn't been invented—is taught routinely to millions of high school students. No one thinks anything of it, but consider what this means. The intellectual content of the material is the same, and people's brains aren't any different; seven hundred and some years isn't nearly enough time for a broad upgrade in human brainpower. Instead, just as in sports, the standard of what we do with what we've got has simply risen tremendously.

When Tchaikovsky finished writing his Violin Concerto in 1878, he asked the famous violinist Leopold Auer to give the premier performance. Auer studied the score and said no—he thought the work was unplayable. Today every young violinist graduating from Juilliard can play it. The music is the same, the violins are the same, and human beings haven't changed. But people have learned how to perform much, much better.

New research shows that the trend is continuing, even in realms where the standard already seems impressively high. For example, a cleverly designed study of world championship games in chess found recently that the game is being played at a far higher level today than it was in the nineteenth century, when the world championship was first contested. Using powerful chess software, the researchers found that former champions made many more tactical errors than today's players do. In fact, champions of yore would about match today's players just below the master level, not even approaching the grand master or champion levels. The researchers concluded, "these results imply dramatic improvements at the highest level of intellectual achievement in the game of chess over the last two centuries." Again, the game hasn't changed, and not enough time has passed for human brains to have changed. What has changed is that people are doing much more with what they've got.

In business it's overwhelmingly clear that standards of performance will continue to rise more relentlessly than they have in the past, thus increasing the value of great performance. The most important reason is that infotech has given customers unprecedented power, and with that power they're demanding more. We all understand this because we've all bought stuff online. As buyers, we receive more information than we could ever see before. We know what the car dealer paid for the car. We know what prescription drugs cost in Canada. We know that a college textbook costing $135 in the campus bookstore can be ordered for $70 from England. And what we know and save as consumers is nothing compared with what corporate buyers know about their suppliers, and the cost savings it has suddenly become possible to squeeze out of them. As the strategy consultant Gary Hamel likes to say, if customer ignorance is a profit center for you, you're in trouble.

The Challenge We All Face

It isn't just companies that have to keep kicking up their performance more than they ever did before. It's each of us individually. The pressure on us to keep getting better is greater than it used to be because of a historic change in the economy.

To understand what's going on, we need to take a step back. How many offers of credit cards do you get in the mail every day? Do your kids get them? How about your pet? (It has happened.) Maybe you also receive unsolicited checks with your name and address printed in the corner, and a letter urging you to write out those checks to pay some bills. It's happening because the world's financial institutions are awash in money. They literally have more than they know what to do with, and they're saying: Take some, please!

Those financial institutions aren't alone. Companies of all kinds have far more money than they need. The cash held by U.S. companies is hitting all-time records. Companies are using some of this money to buy back their own stock at record rates. When a company does this, it's saying to its investors: We don't have any good ideas for what to do with this, so here—maybe you do.

These are all manifestations of a much larger phenomenon. For roughly five hundred years—from the explosion of commerce and wealth that accompanied the Renaissance until the late twentieth century—the scarce resource in business was financial capital. If you had it, you had the means to create more wealth, and if you didn't, you didn't. That world is now gone. Today, in a change that is historically quite sudden, financial capital is abundant. The scarce resource is no longer money. It's human ability.

Such assertions run the danger of sounding like up-with-people fluff, so it's important to demonstrate that they're true. Fortunately, the evidence is easy to spot. It has become possible in recent years to create staggering amounts of shareholder wealth with business models that use very little financial capital but tons of human capital. For example, Microsoft has used about $30 billion of financial capital from all sources over its corporate lifetime, and it has created about $221 billion of shareholder wealth. By contrast, Procter & Gamble, one of the best managed and most admired companies in the world, has used far more capital than Microsoft, about $83 billion, yet has created much less shareholder wealth—about $126 billion.

Even more dramatically, Google has used only about $5 billion of capital but has created about $124 billion of shareholder wealth. Contrast that with, say, PepsiCo, another superbly managed company built on a business model from an earlier age; using much more financial capital than Google, about $34 billion, it has created much less shareholder wealth, about $73 billion.

Microsoft and Google understand perfectly well that their success is built on human capital. Both companies are famous for the scorching intelligence of the people they hire and for the brutally rigorous tests they impose on job applicants. Bill Gates has said that if you took the twenty smartest people out of Microsoft it would be an insignificant company, and if you ask around the company what its core competency is, they don't say anything about software. They say it's hiring. They know what the scarce resource is.

What makes this phenomenon so significant is that it applies to all companies, not just infotech wonders. Consider the most extreme case of a company that would appear to rely almost entirely on financial capital, Exxon Mobil. It's the largest company in the world, and its business is arguably the world's most capital-intensive. In recent years it has been investing about $20 billion a year in its business, the largest capital investment program of any company in the world. But it has been giving even more—$33 billion in 2006—back to the shareholders through dividends and stock buybacks, the largest-ever example of "Here—maybe you can do something with this." I asked the CEO, Rex Tillerson, why he followed that policy. After all, Exxon earns tremendous returns on the money it invests, far better than any of its major competitors. So why not build shareholder wealth by investing more than $20 billion a year? The constraint, he says, isn't money, it's people: "You don't just walk out on the street and hire an Exxon Mobil engineer or geoscientist or researcher." He could fund more projects, but he doesn't have enough qualified people to manage them.

For virtually every company, the scarce resource today is human ability. That's why companies are under unprecedented pressure to make sure that every employee is as highly developed as possible—and as we shall see, no one knows what the limits of development are.

At the same time, a separate historic trend is putting individuals under unprecedented pressure to develop their own abilities more highly than was ever necessary before, quite apart from anything their employers may or may not do to develop them. That trend is the advent of the first large-scale global labor market. We've had global product markets for centuries and global capital markets for almost as long. But labor markets were different. For most of human history, most work

13

has been place-based. Often it was tied to the location of customers; farriers had to be where the horses were, bakers where the buyers were, bankers where the depositors and borrowers were. Other work was tied to the location of the natural resources on which it relied. Miners had to be where the coal was, fishermen where the fish were. Detroit became the car capital because it was the best spot at which to bring together, via rail and Great Lakes shipping, the coal, steel, rubber, and other components of a car, and from which to distribute to the nation.

Offshoring happened for decades, but for most of that time it wasn't a national obsession because it didn't happen much; before the info age, coordinating production in a foreign country was slow and cumbersome. Thus the great majority of workers competed for jobs mostly with other workers in their area, and when they competed more broadly, it was mostly with workers in other parts of the country.

But today, many millions of workers in developed economies compete for jobs with other workers around the world. The reason is that a large and growing proportion of all work is information-based and doesn't involve moving or processing anything physical at all. We're all familiar with some of the results: workers in other countries answering our customer service calls, reading our X-rays, writing our software. Other developments may be more surprising. More than a million American tax returns are prepared in India each year. A major accounting firm audited a client company in London by flying in a team of accountants from India, putting them up in a hotel for three weeks, and flying them back; it was much cheaper than using British accountants.

It's all happening because the costs of computing power and telecommunications are in free fall. Processing information and moving it around costs practically nothing. For those same reasons, offshoring of manufacturing jobs is also exploding. Coordinating global supply chains has become so fast and precise that it's now worthwhile to take advantage of cheaper labor that happens to be halfway around the world.

The result is that a fast-growing number of workers everywhere have to be just as good—and just as good a value—as the very best workers in their field anywhere on earth. It's true that a few jobs can probably escape this brutal competition, but not as many as we're tempted to think. You might suppose, for example, that dentists will always have to be where their patients are. Not so. Many consumers in Britain, where dentistry is a much-criticized part of the National Health Service, are taking low-fare flights to Poland to get their dental work done by well-trained dentists who charge bargain prices.

If you think your job isn't exportable, you may be right—but think about it hard before you relax.

"World class" is a term that gets thrown around too easily. For most of history, few people had to worry about what world class was. But now that's changing. In a global, information-based, interconnected economy, businesses and individuals are increasingly going up against the world's best. The costs of being less than truly world class are growing, as are the rewards of being genuinely great.

Understanding where extraordinary performance comes from would be valuable at any time. Now it's crucial.

It must also be said that the value of better understanding great performance is more than just economic. Not that there's anything wrong with prosperity; most people want to be better off, and helping them keep their jobs, fund their retirements, and pay for their kids' educations—by helping them become better performers—can prevent a lot of human suffering. But there's more to life than work, and there's more to be good at than your job.

Being good at whatever we want to do—playing the violin, running a race, painting a picture, leading a group of people—is among the deepest sources of fulfillment we will ever know. Most of what we want to do is hard. That's life. Encountering problems, discouragement, and disappointment is inevitable. So any knowledge about what makes us better at the things we want to do—real knowledge, not myth or conjecture—can be used not just to make us richer but also to make us happier.

Researchers have uncovered and refined a great deal of such knowledge over the past thirty years, and it holds tremendous promise for making us better at undertakings of every kind. This knowledge has not been widely dispersed or well understood, which makes the opportunity of applying it all the greater. Many of the findings are surprising; in fact, though they're ultimately full of promise and even inspiration, many people resist them at first.

The nineteenth-century humorist Josh Billings famously said, "It ain't so much the things we don't know that get us into trouble. It's the things we know that just ain't so." The first step in understanding the new findings on great performance is using them to help us identify what we know for sure that just ain't so.

Chapter Two

Talent Is Overrated

Confronting the unexpected facts about innate abilities

In 1992, a small group of researchers in England went looking for talent. They couldn't find it.

They were looking for musical talent, which made sense, because that's the kind people feel most certain about. They know it exists. They know there's a reason why they can't sing and other people can, or why Mozart could write symphonies when he was a teenager, or why some people can play the piano beautifully as mere children while others struggle to play a scale. Most people simply know that certain lucky individuals are born with a talent for music, and that's the main factor in how well they perform it or write it.

When researchers in a separate study polled a sample consisting mainly of education professionals, more than 75 percent believed that singing, composing, and playing concert instruments requires a special gift or talent; that 75 percent is a higher proportion than those who believe particular talent is necessary in any other field.

So the researchers looked at 257 young people, all of whom had been introduced to the study of music but who otherwise varied widely. They were classified into five ability groups, ranging from students at a music school who were admitted by competitive audition (the top group) to students who had tried an instrument for at least six months but had given it up. Researchers matched the groups by age, gender, instruments, and socioeconomic class.

Then the researchers interviewed the students and their parents at length. How much did the kids practice? At what age could they first sing a recognizable tune? And so on. Fortunately for the researchers, the British educational system gave them an independent means of assessing these students beyond the five ability groups used. A national system of grading young instrumentalists is rigorous and uniform; the great majority of kids studying instruments take graded exams that are formulated and conducted by a national panel of assessors, who then place each student into one of nine grades.

This setup let the researchers check their results two ways as they tried to figure out what accounted for the wide difference in musical ability and achievement among their 257 subjects.

The results were clear. The telltale signs of precocious musical ability in the top-performing groups—the evidence of talent that we all know exists—simply weren't there. On the contrary, judged by early signs of special talent, all the groups were highly similar. The top group, the students at music school, were superior on one measure of early ability—the ability to repeat a tune; they could do that at the age of eighteen months, on average, versus about twenty-four months for the others. But it's hard to regard even that as evidence of special talent, because the interviews revealed that the parents of these kids were far more active in singing to them than other parents were. On several other dimensions the various groups of students showed no significant differences; they all started studying their main instrument around age eight, for example.

Still, the students obviously differed dramatically in their musical accomplishments, and even if extensive interviewing turned up no evidence of particular talent, weren't the differing levels of achievement in themselves evidence of talent? What else could it be? As it happens, the study produced an answer to that question. One factor, and only one factor, predicted how musically accomplished the students were, and that was how much they practiced.

Specifically, the researchers studied the results of those nationally administered grade-level exams. You would expect, of course, that the students who went on to win places at the music school—and this was a school whose graduates regularly win national competitions and go on to professional music careers—would reach any given grade level more quickly and easily than the students who ended up being less accomplished. That's the very meaning of being musically talented. But it didn't happen. On the contrary: The researchers calculated the average hours of practice needed by the most elite group of students to reach each grade level, and they calculated the average hours needed by each of the other groups. There were no statistically significant differences. For students who ended up going to the elite music school as well as for students who just played casually for fun, it took an average of twelve hundred hours of practice to reach grade 5, for example. The music school students reached grade levels at earlier ages than the other students for the simple reason that they practiced more each day.

By age twelve, the researchers found, the students in the most elite group were practicing an average of two hours a day versus about fifteen minutes a day for the students in the lowest group, an 800 percent difference. So students could put in their hours a little bit each day or a lot each day, but nothing, it turned out, enabled any group to reach any given grade level without putting in those hours. As one of the researchers, Professor John A. Sloboda of the University of Keele, put it: "There is absolutely no evidence of a 'fast track' for high achievers."

To put the results in their starkest terms: Shown five groups of students, one of which won positions at a top-ranked music school and one of which gave up even trying to play an instrument, we would all say the first group is obviously immensely more talented than the latter. But the study showed that—at least as most of us understand "talent," meaning an ability to achieve more easily—they were not.

What Is Talent?

If it turns out that we're all wrong about talent—and I will offer a lot more evidence that we are—that's a big problem. If we believe that people without a particular natural talent for some activity will never be very good at it, or at least will never be competitive with those who possess that talent, then we'll direct them away from that activity. We'll tell them they shouldn't even think about it. We'll steer our kids away from particular studies, whether they're art, tennis, economics, or Chinese, because we think we've seen signs that they have no talent in those realms. In business we constantly see managers redirect people's careers based on slender evidence of what they've "got." Most insidiously, in our own lives, we will try something new and, finding that it isn't easy for us, conclude that we have no talent for it, and so we never pursue it.

Thus our views about talent, which are extremely deeply held, are extraordinarily important for the future of our lives, our children's lives, our companies, and the people in them. Understanding the reality of talent is worth a great deal.

We must be clear about what we mean by the term. People often use it just to mean excellent performance or to describe those who are terrific performers. "The Red Sox have a lot of talent in the outfield" means only that the outfielders are very good. "The war for talent," a popular topic in business and the title of a book, means the fight to attract good performers. In the TV business, "talent" is the generic term for anyone who appears on camera. "Get the talent on set!" just means get the performers to their places; anyone who watches much TV realizes that in this case the term is totally nonjudgmental.

None of those meanings is the critical one. When the term is used in ways that change the courses of people's lives, it has a specific meaning. It is a natural ability to do something better than most people can do it. That something is fairly specific—play golf, sell things, compose music, lead an organization. It can be spotted early, before the ability is fully expressed. And it is innate; you're born with it, and if you're not born with it, you can't acquire it.

By this definition, most of us believe that talent exists in practically every field. Listen carefully to your next conversation about music, sports, and games; it's difficult to talk about participants for more than two sentences without invoking "talent." In other realms the concept is never far away. Russell Baker, the great former *New York Times* columnist, believed he was born with "the word gene," a writer in the making literally from birth. In business, we commonly say that Bob is a natural salesman, or Jean is a born leader, or Pat has a head for figures. Warren Buffett often tells people, "I was hardwired at birth to allocate capital," which is his way of saying he came into this world with an ability to spot winning investments.

We're all sure that talent exists, but that doesn't mean we've really thought about it. Hardly any of us have done that. The notion is just part of our conception of the world, and it's worth asking why.

Much of the answer resides in an unlikely place, the writings of a nineteenth-century English aristocrat and explorer who never finished college. Francis Galton had believed as a young man that people were born with largely the same capabilities, which were developed to varying degrees during life. Despite the ancient view from mythology and religion that all kinds of gifts were god-given, the idea of equal abilities had become popular by Galton's time. It grew from deep roots in the eighteenth-century notions of equality that fueled the American and French revolutions. Then Thoreau, Emerson, and others told the world that we all possess greater strength and potential than we ever imagined. The evidence flowered in nineteenth-century economic expansion; as trade and industry thrived from Europe to America to Asia, and people found wealth and opportunity on every shore, it seemed everyone could make of themselves what they would.

Galton accepted that view—until he read the works of his cousin,

Charles Darwin. Suddenly Galton's opinion reversed, and he promoted his new theory with a convert's zeal. Indeed, some of his influence—which was enormous and remains so in widely held views on this issue—probably stemmed from the bulldozer confidence with which he wrote. "I have no patience with the hypothesis occasionally expressed, and often implied, especially in tales written to teach children to be good, that babies are born pretty much alike, and that the sole agencies in creating differences between boy and boy, and man and man, are steady application and moral effort," he wrote in his foundational work, *Hereditary Genius* (the possibility that girls or women might merit attention never occurred to him). "It is in the most unqualified manner that I object to pretensions of natural equality."

Galton's view was simple: Just as height and other physical traits tend to be inherited, so does "eminence." He proved his theory, he said, by "showing how large is the number of instances in which men who are more or less illustrious have eminent kinsfolk." By scouring the obituaries in the *Times*, he assembled hundreds of pages of evidence illustrating this tendency among judges, poets, commanders, musicians, painters, "divines," and "wrestlers of the north country," among others. Eminence in particular fields ran in particular families. The ability to achieve such eminence must therefore be inherited, present at birth.

Though it is tempting to smirk at someone who studied eminence among wrestlers of the north country, we must not lampoon Galton. By trying to apply Darwin's ideas to nonphysical human traits, he pushed science forward, and he advanced techniques of statistical correlation and regression that today are essential in all of science. He understood that he was raising deep questions about where greatness comes from. He coined the phrase "nature versus nurture." And he established what he called "natural gifts" as a subject of scientific inquiry, which it has remained to this day, as seen in modern scholarly publications such as the *Journal for the Education of the Gifted* and *Conceptions of Giftedness*.

The idea of giftedness—which is the same as our definition of talent—thus has a very considerable head of steam behind it. But what if the concept itself turns out to be troubled?

Probing the Talent Concept

A number of researchers now argue that giftedness or talent means nothing like what we think it means, if indeed it means anything at all. A few contend that the very existence of talent is not, as they carefully put it, supported by evidence.

Their argument is stronger than we might at first imagine. Many studies of accomplished individuals have tried to figure out the key elements of their achievements, in part by interviewing the individuals and their parents, as in the English music study mentioned earlier. In these studies, all the subjects are people of whom we'd say, "They're very talented." Yet over and over, the researchers found few signs of precocious achievement before the individuals started intensive training. Such signs did occur occasionally, but in the large majority of cases they didn't. We can all think of examples of people who seemed to be highly talented, but when researchers have looked at large numbers of high achievers, at least in certain fields, most of the people who became extremely good in their field did not show early evidence of gifts. Similar findings have turned up in studies of musicians, tennis players, artists, swimmers, and mathematicians. Of course such findings do not prove that talent doesn't exist. But they suggest an intriguing possibility: that if it does, it may be irrelevant.

Once training begins, we would suppose that talent would certainly show itself; after only three piano lessons, little Ashley is playing pieces that other kids need six months to learn. But again, this does not happen reliably in people who go on to achieve a great deal. In a study of outstanding American pianists, for example, you could not have predicted their eventual high level of achievement even after they'd been training intensively for six years; at that point most of them still weren't standing out from their peers. In retrospect, we'd say all of them were "talented," but talent is looking like an odd concept if it hasn't made itself known after six years of hard study.

Even those few cases in which parents do report early, spontaneous signs of talent turn out to be problematic. Various researchers have found cases of children who reportedly spoke or read at extremely early ages, but they then found that the parents were deeply involved in the children's development and stimulation. Given the extraordinarily close relationship between parents and small children, it can be hard to say what originates where. If baby Kevin smooshes paint on a piece of paper in a way that looks to Mom and Dad like a bunny rabbit, they may decide he's an artistic genius and begin nourishing that notion in every way they can find. We've all seen it happen, and in fact research has found that such interactions do result in differing patterns of abilities in children. We'll look into this more deeply in the final chapter.

You might suppose that in the age of genomic research, there should no longer be any question about precisely what's innate and what isn't. Since talent is by definition innate, there should be a gene (or genes) for it. The difficulty is that scientists haven't yet figured out what each of our twenty-thousand-plus genes does. All we can say for the moment is that no specific genes identifying particular talents have been found. It's possible that they will be; scientists could yet find the piano-playing gene or investing gene or accounting gene. But they haven't so far, and evidence we've already seen suggests that finding talent genes may be a long shot. The extreme increases in top levels of performance in a wide range of fields over the past century have happened far too fast to be connected to genetic changes, which require thousands of years. For that reason, it would seem impossible to argue that genes are what make people great at what they do. The most one could say is that if genes exert any influence, it would seem to be much less than the whole explanation for achieving the highest levels of performance.

Talent skeptics are careful to say that the evidence, taken together, doesn't prove that talent is a myth. They allow that further research could eventually show that individual genetic differences are what make the greatest performers so accomplished. But hundreds of studies conducted over decades have failed to show this. On the contrary, the preponderance of them have suggested very powerfully that genetic differences of this particular type—that is, differences that determine the highest levels of performance—don't exist.

What About Mozart?

And yet . . . how can this be? The antitalent argument may sound sensible at each step, but at the end we're still left with the job of explaining the transcendent greatness of history's most magical, most enduring performers. And how can one possibly account for staggering, immortal achievement *except* as a mysterious divine gift? In fact, when first presented with the logic of the antitalent thesis, a great many people respond immediately with two simple counterarguments: Mozart and Tiger Woods.

Mozart is the ultimate example of the divine-spark theory of greatness. Composing music at age five, giving public performances as a pianist and violinist at age eight, going on to produce hundreds of works, some of which are widely regarded as ethereally great and treasures of Western culture, all in the brief time before his death at age thirty-five—if that isn't talent, and on a mammoth scale, then nothing is.

The facts are worth examining a little more closely. Mozart's father was of course Leopold Mozart, a famous composer and performer in his own right. He was also a domineering parent who started his son on a program of intensive training in composition and performing at age three. Leopold was well qualified for his role as little Wolfgang's teacher by more than just his own eminence; he was deeply interested in how music was taught to children. While Leopold was only so-so as a musician, he was highly accomplished as a pedagogue. His authoritative book on violin instruction, published the same year Wolfgang was born, remained influential for decades.

So from the earliest age, Wolfgang was receiving heavy instruction from an expert teacher who lived with him. Of course his early compositions still seem remarkable, but they raise some provocative questions. It's interesting to note that the manuscripts are not in the boy's own hand; Leopold always "corrected" them before anyone saw them. It seems noteworthy also that Leopold stopped composing at just the time he began teaching Wolfgang.

In some cases it's clear that the young boy's compositions are not original. Wolfgang's first four piano concertos, composed when he was eleven, actually contain no original music by him. He put them together out of works by other composers. He wrote his next three works of this type, today not classified as piano concertos, at age sixteen; these also contain no original music but instead are arrangements of works by Johann Christian Bach, with whom Wolfgang had studied in London. Mozart's earliest symphonies, brief works written when he was just eight, hew closely to the style of Johann Christian Bach, with whom he was studying when they were written.

None of these works is regarded today as great music or even close. They are rarely performed or recorded except as novelties, of interest only because of Mozart's later fame. They seem instead to be the works of someone being trained as a composer by the usual methods—copying, arranging, and imitating the works of others—with the resulting products brought to the world's attention (and just maybe polished a bit) by a father who spent much of his life promoting his son. Mozart's first work regarded today as a masterpiece, with its status confirmed by the number of recordings available, is his Piano Concerto No. 9, composed when he was twenty-one. That's certainly an early age, but we must remember that by then Wolfgang had been through eighteen years of extremely hard, expert training.

This is worth pausing to consider. Any divine spark that Mozart may have possessed did not enable him to produce world-class work quickly or easily, which is something we often suppose a divine spark will do.

Mozart's method of composing was not quite the wonder it was long thought to be. For nearly two hundred years many people have believed that he had a miraculous ability to compose entire major pieces in his head, after which writing them down was mere clerical work. That view was based on a famous letter in which he says as much: "the whole, though it be long, stands almost finished and complete in my mind . . . the committing to paper is done quickly enough . . . and it rarely differs on paper from what it was in my imagination."

That report certainly does portray a superhuman performer. The trouble is, this letter is a forgery, as many scholars later established. Mozart did not conceive whole works in his mind, perfect and complete. Surviving manuscripts show that Mozart was constantly revising, reworking, crossing out and rewriting whole sections, jotting down fragments and putting them aside for months or years. Though it makes the results no less magnificent, he wrote music the way ordinary humans do.

Recent scholarship has put his abilities as a prodigy performer in a new perspective as well. Researchers constructed a "precocity index" for pianists; they figured out the number of years of study needed by a pianist under modern training programs before publicly performing various works, and then compared that with the number of years actually needed by several prodigies throughout history. If the average music student needs six years of preparation before publicly playing a piece, and a given prodigy did it after three years, that student would have an index of 200 percent. Mozart's index is around 130 percent, clearly ahead of average students. But twentieth-century prodigies score 300 percent to 500 percent. This is another example of rising standards. The effects of today's improved training methods apparently swamp the effects of Mozart's genius as a performer.

To repeat, these facts obviously don't affect our regard for Mozart's music. But they drain a lot of the magic and romance out of how it was created, and some people don't like that. In a paper titled "Mozart as a Working Stiff," Mozart scholar Neal Zaslaw describes what happened when he suggested at a Mozart conference in Vienna that the adult composer was focused on turning out product because he needed the money and rarely if ever wrote a work for which he wasn't being paid. "I was quite taken aback at the vehemence with which my remarks were attacked," he recalls. "The moderator of the session took it upon himself to denounce me from the chair." The offense was suggesting that Mozart was merely a human performer with human motivations, not a demigod propelled solely by the divine spark.

That incident raises a significant issue that recurs in judging the greatness of anyone whose field is creative and artistic. We can measure quite precisely the achievements of athletes, chess players, and others whose work can be evaluated objectively. In the world of finance, fund managers and other investors are judged by criteria that can be carried to several decimal places. Even scientists can be judged fairly objectively, if not too precisely, by the influence of their work in the years after it was done. But composers, painters, poets, and other creators are judged by standards that inevitably shift, so we must at least be careful in drawing conclusions based on their greatness. Some artists have been celebrated in their lifetimes and then forgotten by posterity; others were ignored in life and "discovered" only later. J. S. Bach's *St. Matthew Passion,* now widely regarded as one of the greatest musical works ever written, was apparently performed only twice in his lifetime; though the fact strikes us today as incredible, Bach's music in general was not especially esteemed after his death until Felix Mendelssohn championed it decades later. (Mendelssohn's own music would be widely scorned after his death, though it's highly popular today.) The important point is that if we had been studying greatness in 1810, we probably wouldn't have paid much attention to Bach, or in 1910 to

Mendelssohn. As for Mozart, the angry moderator of Zaslaw's panel insisted that Mozart's music could not even be compared with that of his contemporaries because it "belonged only to the highest spheres of creativity." To which Zaslaw responded that "Mozart's music ascended into the higher ether only in the course of the nineteenth century. During his lifetime, it was right down on the ground along with that of the other composers."

Regarding how he produced this music, however it's evaluated, the *New Yorker*'s music critic, Alex Ross, sums up much of the recent scholarship on the Miracle of Salzburg: "Ambitious parents who are currently playing the 'Baby Mozart' video for their toddlers may be disappointed to learn that Mozart became Mozart by working furiously hard."

And Tiger?

Researchers on great performance sometimes call Tiger Woods the Mozart of golf, and the parallels do seem striking. Woods's father, Earl, was a teacher, specifically a teacher of young men, and he had a lifelong passion for sports. He spent the first half of his career in the army, where, he says, his assignments included teaching military history, tactics, and war games to cadets at the City College of New York. In high school and college (Kansas State) he had been a star baseball player, and in the time between college and the army he would coach Little League teams "and take them to the state tournament," he wrote in a little-noticed book, *Training a Tiger*, published shortly before Tiger turned pro. "I love to teach," he said.

Earl had plenty of time to teach his son and was intensely focused on doing so. His wife Kultida and their son, Tiger, were Earl's second family. He had married young and had three children with his first wife, but that marriage ended in divorce. By the time Tiger came along, Earl's previous children were grown, he had retired from the army, and at age forty-four he was working for McDonnell Douglas in Southern

California. He was also fanatical about golf. He had been introduced to the game only a couple of years earlier but had worked extremely hard at it and had achieved a handicap in the low single digits, placing him in the top 10 percent of players. When Tiger was born, Earl wrote, "I had been properly trained and was ready to go. I took over new ground in starting Tiger at an unthinkably early age."

So here's the situation: Tiger is born into the home of an expert golfer and confessed "golf addict" who loves to teach and is eager to begin teaching his new son as soon as possible. Earl's wife does not work outside the home, and they have no other children; they have decided that "Tiger would be the first priority in our relationship," Earl wrote. Earl gives Tiger his first metal club, a putter, at the age of seven months. He sets up Tiger's high chair in the garage, where Earl is hitting balls into a net, and Tiger watches for hours on end. "It was like a movie being run over and over and over for his view," Earl wrote. Earl develops new techniques for teaching the grip and the putting stroke to a student who cannot yet talk. Before Tiger is two, they are at the golf course playing and practicing regularly.

Tiger's prodigious achievements have become well known; he was a local celebrity by the time he reached elementary school and became nationally famous in college. Amid all that has been written about his legend, a couple of facts are especially worth noting. First is the age at which he initially achieved outstanding performance at a level of play involving regular international competition. Let's call it age nineteen, when he was a member of the U.S. team in Walker Cup play (though he did not win his match). At that point he had been practicing golf with tremendous intensity, first under his father and after age four under professional teachers, for seventeen years.

Second, neither Tiger nor his father suggested that Tiger came into this world with a gift for golf. Earl did not believe that Tiger was an ordinary kid (but, then, parents hardly ever believe that). He thought Tiger had an unusual ability to understand what he was told and to keep track of numbers even before he could count very high. Tiger has repeatedly credited his father for his success. Trying to understand his early interest in the game, he has not invoked an inborn fascination. Rather, he has written, "golf for me was an apparent attempt to emulate the person I looked up to more than anyone: my father." Asked to explain Tiger's phenomenal success, father and son always gave the same reason: hard work.

One of Tiger's boyhood coaches later recalled that, on first seeing him, "I felt he was like Mozart." As indeed he was.

In Search of Business Talent

If the concept of specific talents turns out to be troublesome in music and sports, it's even more so in business. We all tend to assume that business giants must possess some special gift for what they do, but evidence turns out to be extremely elusive. In fact, the overwhelming impression that comes from examining the early lives of business greats is just the opposite—that they didn't seem to hold any identifiable gift or give any early indication of what they would become.

To consider a few of the most prominent examples: Jack Welch, named by *Fortune* magazine as the twentieth century's manager of the century, showed no particular inclination toward business, even into his midtwenties. He grew up as a high-achieving kid in Salem, Massachusetts, getting good grades, though "no one would have accused me of being brilliant," he later wrote, and becoming captain of his high school's hockey and golf teams. It was a good enough record to get him into an Ivy League college, but his family couldn't afford it, and he ended up going to the University of Massachusetts. He majored not in business or economics but in chemical engineering. He then went to the University of Illinois and got a master's and a Ph.D. in the same field. As he approached the real world at age twenty-five, he still wasn't sure of his direction and interviewed for faculty jobs at Syracuse and

West Virginia universities. He finally decided to accept an offer to work in a chemical development operation at General Electric.

If anything in Welch's history to that point suggests that he would become the most influential business manager of his time, it's tough—in fact, impossible—to spot it.

Bill Gates, the world's richest human and symbol of a fundamental economic revolution, is a more promising prospect for those who want to explain success through talent. He became fascinated by computers as a kid and says he wrote his first piece of software at age thirteen; it was a program that played tic-tac-toe. Gates and his friend Paul Allen, with whom he later founded Microsoft, were constantly contriving ways to get more computer time on the big clunky machines of the day. They started a business, Traf-O-Data, to build computers that would analyze the data from traffic monitors on city streets; Gates says the device worked, but nobody bought it. After going off to Harvard, he remained immersed in the exciting and fast-changing world of computers.

It's clear that Gates's early interests led directly to Microsoft. The problem is that nothing in his story suggests extraordinary abilities. As he is the first to note, legions of kids were interested in the possibilities of computers in those days. Harvard at that time was bursting with computer geeks who well understood that a technology revolution was happening. What suggested that Gates would become the king of them all? The answer is, nothing in particular. On close examination, it was probably not his software expertise that was most critical to his success. The more relevant abilities were the ability to launch a business and then the quite different abilities required to manage a large corporation. And Traf-O-Data notwithstanding, one looks in vain for signs of those abilities in world-class proportions, or at all, in the young Gates.

In surveying the world's business titans we find Welch-like stories more often than Gates-like stories, lacking even a hint of inclination toward the fields or traits that would one day lead to fame and riches. One of Gates's predecessors as the world's richest man, John D. Rockefeller, illustrates the point. He grew up as a poor, pious boy, hardwork-ing, notable mainly for his seriousness and maturity. But as his most distinguished biographer, Ron Chernow, observes, "In many respects John was forgettable and indistinguishable from many other boys. When he later dazzled the world, many former neighbors and class-mates struggled to summon up even a fuzzy image of him." One thing many acquaintances did recall was young John's firmly stated intention to become rich. But then, Chernow notes, "There was nothing unusual about Rockefeller's boyhood dreams, for the times were feeding avari-cious fantasies in millions of susceptible schoolboys." The most typical assessment seems to come from a woman who tutored the Rockefeller children and later recalled, "I have no recollection of John excelling at anything. I do remember he worked hard at everything; not talking much, and studying with great industry."

Over and over we find these stories of the early life that tell us noth-ing of what's to come, sometimes in even more extreme form. David Ogilvy, regarded by many as the greatest advertising executive of the twentieth century, was expelled from Oxford, slaved in a hotel kitchen in Paris, sold stoves in Scotland, and farmed in Pennsylvania, among many other apparently random occupations that consumed the first seventeen years of his career. Predicting that he would make his mark as an advertising legend would have been difficult, considering that he presented precious little evidence that he would make any mark at all.

But what about Warren Buffett, yet another of the world's richest men, quoted earlier as saying he was born to allocate capital? He showed not only early signs of interest in his eventual field of emi-nence, like Gates, but also precocity. As a boy, Buffett was intensely in-terested in learning about business and investing, and he wanted to make money. He ran several newspaper routes, and at age eleven he bought his first stock, Cities Service preferred. At fifteen, he and a friend bought a used pinball machine and installed it in a barbershop; within a few months they'd added two more machines. Buffett used his profits to buy forty acres of farmland, which he rented to farmers. He was also known as a kid who could add large numbers in his head, and he graduated from high school at sixteen. Later, in graduate school at Columbia, he studied under the famous investing authority Benjamin Graham and received the only A+ that Graham ever awarded.

Buffett's achievements as an investor are world famous, and his story makes it easy to understand why he and many others would say he was born to do what he did. But that explanation—an inborn ability to allocate capital—is not the only way or even the easiest way to account for his success. Buffett's early obsessive interest in money seems unsurprising in someone growing up in the Midwest in the Depression. Similarly, his fascination with stocks and investing is not especially intriguing when one considers that his father was a stockbroker and investor whom young Warren adored. Warren went to work in his father's office at age eleven and thus began learning about investing at a very early age. Yet there's little if any evidence that, even into his early twenties, he was especially good at it. For a while in his teens he was an enthusiastic "chartist," trying to predict the movements of stock prices by studying charts of past movements; research has shown this technique to be worthless as a way to beat the market (though, like many ineffective techniques, it still has believers). Later he tried to be a market timer, choosing the perfect moments to get into and out of stocks; this strategy also is a guaranteed loser over time, and Buffett couldn't make it work.

When Buffett graduated from Columbia Business School, he was such a devotee of his professor, Graham, that he volunteered to work for Graham's investment company for free. But, as Buffett tells the story, "Ben made his customary calculation of value to price and said no." Buffett did go to work for Graham's firm a couple of years later, staying for two years, and then went back to Omaha to start his first investment partnership at age twenty-five.

So at this point we have a picture of a young man who had shown an intense interest in money and investing from an early age and who (like Rockefeller) possessed a powerful compulsion to become rich. He had worked extremely hard at learning all about the field that obsessed him. But he had not yet achieved anything even approaching extraordinary real-world performance. By the time Buffett began accumulating a world-class record of performance, he was well into his thirties—and had been working diligently in his chosen field for more than twenty years.

Still—there were lots of stockbrokers' sons in the Depression, and only one of them became Warren Buffett. Why? That's a large and deep question that we'll examine further; the key point for the moment is that the concept of innate business talent is not looking like a very promising answer to the question of how Buffett or any of the business greats became who they were.

More generally, it seems we need to recalibrate our views on the role of specific, innate talents. We need not be absolutists about the matter. Heated arguments over whether such talents exist at all are best left to the scholarly researchers. For most of us, the critically important point is that, at the very least, these talents are much less important than we usually think. They seem not to play the crucial role that we generally assign to them, and it's far from clear what role they do play. In chapters 4, 5, 6, 9, and 10, I will share much more evidence on this matter.

But even if we have to admit that the case for the central role of specific talent is weak, we may still believe that great achievement requires exceptional, and inborn, general abilities. You don't reach the high elevations of any field without an IQ that's off the charts or an XXL memory. Or so we tend to assume. But this belief also, deep-seated though it may be, is worth closer examination.

Chapter Three

How Smart Do You Have to Be?

*The true role of intelligence and memory
in high achievement*

On July 11, 1978, in a psychology lab at Carnegie Mellon University in Pittsburgh, an undergraduate who would become known in the scientific literature as SF sat trying to remember a list of random numbers. He was a subject in an experiment being conducted by Professor William Chase, a famous researcher in psychology, and a postdoctoral fellow named Anders Ericsson. They were testing SF and other subjects on a standard memory test known as the digit span task: A researcher reads a list of random digits at the rate of one per second; after a pause of twenty seconds, the subject then repeats as many digits, in order, as he or she can remember. Psychologists had been running this test on subjects for many years. What was so interesting about SF was the extraordinary number of digits he could recall.

If you're like most people, you'll max out at around seven numbers on the digit span task. You may get to nine, but going further is rare. (It's harder than remembering a phone number; try it.) Another of Chase and Ericsson's subjects had been tested an hour a day for nine days and had never gone beyond nine digits; he had dropped out of the study, insisting no further improvement was possible. In a much earlier study, two subjects had managed to increase their digit span to fourteen after many hours of testing. But on this day, SF was being asked to recall twenty-two digits, a new record. The toll it was taking on him was large.

"All right, all right, all right," he muttered after Ericsson read him the list. "All right! All right. Oh . . . geez!" He clapped his hands loudly three times, then grew quiet and seemed to focus further. "Okay. Okay. . . . Four-thirteen-point-one!" he yelled. He was breathing heavily. *"Seventy-seven eighty-four!"* He was nearly screaming. *"Oh six oh three!"* Now he was screaming. *"Four-nine-four, eight-seven-oh!"* Pause. *"Nine-forty-six!"* Screeching now. Only one digit left. But it isn't there. *"Nine-forty-six-point . . . Oh, nine-forty-six-point . . ."* He was screaming and sounding desperate. Finally, hoarse and strangled: *"TWO!"*

He had done it. As Ericsson and Chase checked the results, there came a knock on the door. It was the campus police. They'd had a report of someone screaming in the lab area.

What SF Started

SF's achievement was significant in a couple of ways. His record of twenty-two digits didn't stand for long. He kept setting new records (soon without screaming), until eventually, after about 250 hours of training over a period of two years, he could recall eighty-two digits. To appreciate what that means, imagine someone reading you the following list of numbers, one per second:

8 3 7 2 6 8 9 2 7 8 6 2 7 9 2 5 0 8 9 8 3 6 8 4 0 8 0 4 2 6 2 8 9 1 9 9 9 6 3 9 2 7 7 8 2 1 3 4 3 1 7 1 8 9 6 5 1 8 2 4 6 5 7 5 2 9 1 4 4 5 2 6 4 3 7 8 5 3 5 0 8 7

Keeping that list in your head, in order, after hearing it once would seem simply impossible. Yet SF's memory, when tested, had been average before he began training. His grades were very good, but his intelligence, when measured by standardized tests, was average. Nothing about him suggested that he would ever achieve amazing feats of memory.

In addition, while he stopped training at 82 digits, nothing in his progress to that point indicated that he had reached his limit. In fact, a friend of his who later became a research subject of Chase and Ericsson reached 102 digits, with no indication that he had reached his limit. Chase and Ericsson concluded, "There is apparently no limit to improvements in memory skill with practice."

That was the first significance of SF—showing that a person of average general abilities could nonetheless extend one of those abilities to levels that would seem unimaginable. How he did it turned out to be critically important, as we shall see.

The second significance was that the experiment planted a seed in the mind of Anders Ericsson, who would go on to become the preeminent researcher in the field of great performance. For him, SF exemplified what he calls "the remarkable potential of 'ordinary' adults and their amazing capacity for change with practice." That is the theme of his research over the past thirty years. It has taken him far beyond the study of memory, but it's appropriate that that's where it began, because memory, along with general intelligence, is widely regarded as a key skill of great performers.

What Does "Smart" Mean?

That's especially true in business. For example, former GE chief Jack Welch was famous for seeming to remember everything about one of the world's largest and most complicated companies, the kind of guy who could spot an inconsistency on the twenty-sixth line of a financial statement during an operating review that was glazing everyone else's eyes. Such stories are quite common among preeminent executives. A generation earlier, Harold Geneen of ITT was legendary for the same ability.

Besides prodigious memories, high-performing businesspeople often seem to have tremendous intellects. Warren Buffett is famous for doing complicated math in his head. He claims not to own a calculator, and given his reputation for honesty, there's no reason to doubt him. Steve Ross, who built the Warner Communications empire before selling it to Time Inc., was known for analyzing complex deals in his head and considered this ability a personal competitive advantage. He supposedly said, "I hate calculators. They're the equalizer." Andy Grove, the great former CEO of Intel, radiates intellect and was known to give little slack to subordinates who couldn't keep up. The same is true of Barry Diller, who built exceptional careers in television, movies, and the Internet.

Even if we're prepared to question the notion that certain people come into this world with specific gifts for business, most of us still assume that the greats possess tremendous general abilities, especially intelligence and memory. We see individuals—Welch, Buffett, and many others—who seem to prove the point, and plenty of other examples as well. Goldman Sachs, the most highly regarded firm on Wall Street, has long been known for hiring only the smartest graduates of the most elite schools. McKinsey & Company, the king of consulting firms, regularly hires most of the Baker Scholars—the most outstanding students—at the Harvard Business School. Microsoft and Google are famous for grilling job applicants with questions that would leave most people begging for mercy. Everywhere we see hypersuccessful companies seemingly filled with people who got perfect scores on their SATs.

So it's definitely surprising, at least at first, to find that research doesn't support the view that extraordinary natural general abilities—as distinct from developed abilities like SF's memory—are necessary for high achievement. In fact, in a wide range of fields, including business, the connection between general intelligence and specific abilities is weak and in some cases apparently nonexistent. As for memory, the whole concept of a powerful memory is problematic because it turns out that memory ability is very clearly created rather than innate.

Obviously the most successful people in business or any other domain have something special. But what is it? The idea that it's an inborn gift for cost accounting or writing software or trading cocoa futures doesn't seem to hold up. Harder to believe is that it isn't even more general cognitive abilities. That's what the research is telling us, but it's so counterintuitive that it requires some explanation.

We begin by delving briefly into the heavily fraught and extremely deep concept of intelligence. What do we mean when we say someone is smart? It's one of those concepts that we understand intuitively, but then we dwell on it and realize how complicated it is. Some people seem smart with numbers, others with words, others with abstract concepts, still others with concrete knowledge, and how do all those kinds of smart fit together? It seems likely that if we sat down and thought about it, most of us would come up with a basic definition of smart that parallels closely the much maligned concept of IQ.

Tests of IQ, as they have been developed over the past century, actually consist of ten subtests that try to capture various aspects of intelligence (the subtests focus on information, arithmetic, vocabulary, comprehension, picture completion, block design, object assembly, coding, picture arrangement, and similarities). After giving these tests to millions of people, researchers have found that performance on the subtests is correlated, that is, people who perform well on one of the subtests tend to perform well on all of them. Why? The researchers hypothesized that there must be some general factor that influences performance on all the subtests, and they called this factor general intelligence, or g. That's what IQ measures.

An assortment of academics and nonspecialists have been beating up on IQ for years, largely because of what it doesn't measure and doesn't explain, and many of these attacks are justified. For example, critical thinking is obviously important in the real world, and IQ doesn't measure it. Ditto with social skills, honesty, tolerance, wisdom, and other traits that we value and would love to understand better; they're not on the IQ test. In response, writers and researchers over the years have proposed new concepts of what they call other types of intelligence. Most notable is Harvard professor Howard Gardner, whose theory of multiple intelligences (linguistic, musical, visual/spatial, and at least five others) has been highly influential. Daniel Goleman has written best-selling books on what he calls emotional intelligence, or EQ—the many factors (self-control, zeal, persistence, and others) that seem to contribute to success in real-world relationships from marriage to the workplace. These concepts can be highly useful, although calling them types of intelligence may not be, because it fuzzes up the concept of intelligence. One of the most famous intelligence researchers, Arthur Jensen, has said it's like calling chess an athletic skill. We certainly want to study chess, but classifying it in that way may only slow down our understanding of where athletic skill comes from.

So for the moment we stick with the concept of general intelligence as *g,* measured by IQ. It has a pretty good record. It predicts fairly well (though far from perfectly) how people will perform in school. Professor James R. Flynn, an eminent intelligence researcher, reports that people in professional, managerial, and technical jobs have an above-average IQ as a group. Among workers overall, average IQ increases with the complexity of the work, which seems totally unsurprising. It supports what most of us would suppose: Smarter people do better. Research says they do more demanding work and achieve higher socio-economic status. When we think of intelligence in the general, old-fashioned, academic sense, then particle physicists are smarter than dentists, who are smarter than assembly-line workers, on average. So a mass of evidence seems to undergird the view that even if the world's great performers don't possess a specific, targeted gift, they still have some more general natural advantage, most likely superior intelligence.

The trouble starts when we dig beneath the averages. Consider your own acquaintances. You are virtually guaranteed to know people who have succeeded in the business world, sometimes very considerably, without evincing conventional brainpower that's in any way impressive. We typically explain this by saying they're good with people, or they work extremely hard, or they really put their heart into it. Such factors may relate to Gardner's multiple "intelligences" or Goleman's EQ, but the critical point is that whatever these people have, it definitely is not general intelligence—our first hint that IQ may not explain great performance as well as we usually suspect it might.

The evidence is actually far more substantial than our own random experiences. A wide range of research shows that the correlations between IQ and achievement aren't nearly as strong as the data on broad averages would suggest, and in many cases there's no correlation at all.

Consider, for example, a study of salespeople. This was a so-called meta-analysis, the largest of its type ever conducted, gathering data from several dozen previous studies looking at almost forty-six thousand individuals. Studying businesspeople in the real world is tough because you generally can't control the conditions, and the results are often unclear; whether a decision was good or bad may not be known for years. Salespeople make attractive subjects for researchers because at least they produce something clear to measure: sales. There may still be endless sources of noise in the results, as salespeople explain eloquently to their bosses, but over time and over large numbers of subjects, most of that should wash out.

In this analysis of analyses, the researchers found that if you ask salespeople's bosses to rate them, the ratings track intelligence moderately well; bosses tend to think that smarter salespeople are better. But when the researchers compared intelligence with actual sales results, they found nothing. Intelligence was virtually useless in predicting how well a salesperson would perform. Whatever it is that makes a sales ace, it seems to be something other than brainpower.

These results are surprising also because they suggest that sales supervisors are deluding themselves. You'd think they would have every incentive to know the objective performance of their subordinates and rate them on that basis, but apparently they do not. That finding has been supported in at least one other large meta-analysis. It seems our view that intelligence necessarily produces better performance is so deep that it may occasionally even blind us to reality.

A more detailed investigation of real-world performance focused on an activity that has a lot in common with business: betting on horses. You study the facts, you estimate odds, and you decide where to put your money; it isn't so different from management. The researchers went to a track and recruited a group of subjects. Based on their ability to forecast post-time odds, these subjects were deemed experts or non-experts. The experts were by definition a lot better at that task, but except for that difference, the two subsets on average turned out to show no significant differences in several ways that you might expect to matter: years of experience at the track, years of formal education, occupational prestige scores, and IQ. The IQ averages and variabilities of both groups, in addition to being the same, were almost exactly the same as for the overall population. The expert forecasters were no smarter than the nonexperts or than people in general.

Looking at the data more closely, the researchers found that knowing a particular subject's IQ was of no use in predicting whether he was a handicapping expert. For example, one of the experts was a construction worker with an IQ of 85 (what one of the early IQ test developers classified as "dull normal") who had been going to the track regularly for sixteen years; he picked the top horse in ten out of ten races the researchers presented and picked the top three horses in correct order five times out of ten. By contrast, one of the nonexperts was a lawyer with an IQ of 118 ("bright normal," almost "superior") who had been going to the track regularly for fifteen years; he picked the top horse in only three of ten races and the top three in only one of ten.

What makes these results especially interesting is that accurately forecasting odds is highly complex. More than a dozen factors have to be considered, and they relate to one another in complicated ways. In fact, the researchers found that the expert handicappers used models that were far more complex than what the nonexperts used, so-called multiplicative models in which the values of some factors (such as track condition) altered the importance of others (such as last-race speed). In other words, what the experts were accomplishing was extremely demanding. And to repeat, IQ just didn't seem to matter. "Low-IQ experts always used more complex models than high-IQ nonexperts," the researchers found. Not only did handicapping expertise fail to correlate with IQ, it didn't even correlate with performance on the arithmetic subtest of the IQ test.

The researchers' conclusion: Their results suggest "that whatever it is that an IQ test measures, it is not the ability to engage in cognitively complex forms of multivariate reasoning." That last phrase is not one that most of us use very often, but it's actually a very good description of what most of us do every day in our working lives, and what the best performers do extremely well. You just don't have to be especially "smart," as traditionally defined, to do it.

Similar results turn up in a wide range of fields. For example, in chess—another realm that businesspeople feel is a lot like their own—IQ does not reliably predict performance. This seems hard to believe, since we generally think of chess as an exercise in pure brainpower. Yet researchers have found that some chess grand masters have IQs that are below normal. It's a similar story with Go, the Japanese game that is at least as complex as chess. Also surprising, some top Scrabble players score below average on tests of verbal ability.

Even when performance does match up with IQ in a way we would expect, the effect tends to be short-lived. That is, even if high-IQ people do better than low-IQ people when first trying a task that's new to them, the relationship tends to get weaker and may eventually disappear completely as they work at the task and get better at it. For example, a study of children who took up chess found that the strength of IQ as a predictor dropped drastically as the children worked and got better, and IQ was of no value in predicting how quickly they would improve. Many studies of adults in the workplace have shown the same pattern. IQ is a decent predictor of performance on an unfamiliar task, but once a person has been at a job for a few years, IQ predicts little or nothing about performance.

None of this suggests there's anything the least bit wrong with being smart if you want to succeed in business or anything else. Many of the most successful people do seem to be highly intelligent. But what the research suggests very strongly is that the link between intelligence and high achievement isn't nearly as powerful as we commonly suppose. Most important, the research tells us that intelligence as we usually think of it—a high IQ—is not a prerequisite to extraordinary achievement.

How's Your Memory?

The evidence is similar when it comes to that other general ability we often associate with hypersuccessful people, an amazing memory. Francis Galton was certain that this was one of those "natural gifts" that characterize "illustrious men" and that you either inherit it or you don't. For example: "[Richard] Porson, the Greek scholar, was remarkable for this gift, and, I may add, the 'Porson memory' was hereditary in that family." Yet a large mass of more recent evidence shows that memory ability is acquired, and it can be acquired by pretty much anyone.

Recall SF, who developed truly remarkable memory ability though he started with only average memory (and average IQ). He did it by working out his own mnemonic system based on his experience as a competitive runner. For example, recall his struggle to remember the final digits of his twenty-two-digit span. He kept saying, "Nine-forty-six-point . . . nine-forty-six-point. . . ." Why was he saying "point"? (And you may have noticed that he also said it earlier in the sequence, "Four-thirteen-point-one.") It's because when he heard the digits 9 4 6 2, he thought of it as 9 minutes, 46.2 seconds, an excellent time for running two miles. Similarly, 4 1 3 1 became 4:13.1, a mile time. This is what researchers call a retrieval structure, which has particular significance that we'll hear more about later. Many other studies since SF have confirmed that apparently average people can achieve extraordinary memory ability by developing their own retrieval structures or being given them by researchers.

A different type of research reinforces the finding that memory is developed, not innate. World-class chess players, in addition to being considered awesomely smart, are generally assumed to have superhuman memories, and with good reason. Champions routinely put on exhibitions in which they play lesser opponents while blindfolded; they hold the entire chessboard in their heads. Some of these exhibitions strike the rest of us as simply beyond belief. The Czech master Richard Réti once played twenty-nine blindfolded games simultaneously. (Afterward he left his briefcase at the exhibition site and commented on what a poor memory he had.) Miguel Najdorf, a Polish-Argentinean grand master, played forty-five blindfolded games simultaneously in São Paulo in 1947; he won thirty-nine, drew four, and lost two.

It's hard to believe that any normal person could do such things. But consider a study in which highly skilled chess players as well as nonplayers were shown chessboards with twenty to twenty-five pieces set up as they were in actual games; the research subjects were shown the boards only briefly—five to ten seconds—and then asked to recall the positions of the pieces. The results were what you'd expect: The chess masters could typically recall the position of every piece, while the nonplayers could place only four or five pieces. Then the researchers repeated the procedure, this time with pieces positioned not as in actual games but randomly. The nonplayers again could place only four or five pieces. But the masters, who had been studying chessboards for most of their lives, did scarcely better, placing only six or seven pieces.

The chess masters did not have incredible memories. What they had was an incredible ability to remember real chess positions.

This research has been repeated with players of Go, Gomoku (a game played with the same board and pieces as Go, but with a different objective), and bridge, and the results are the same. Expert players have vastly superior abilities to remember real game positions, or in bridge, hands arranged in the usual order. But when the boards or hands are mixed up, the experts' memories are just ordinary. Similarly, SF's incredible memory did not extend beyond the specific task he had practiced. When he was read lists of random consonants instead of random digits, his memory was no better than yours or mine.

In short, the widespread view that highly accomplished people have tremendous memories is in one sense justified—they often astound us with what they can remember. But the view that their amazing ability is a rare natural gift is not justified. Remarkable memory ability is apparently available to anyone.

It may seem surprising that off-the-charts general abilities, especially intelligence and memory, are not necessary for extraordinary achievement, but it becomes less surprising when we consider the qualities that highly successful companies and business leaders look for in employees, or rather what they don't look for. It's certainly true that McKinsey, Goldman Sachs, Microsoft, Google, and other top companies are looking explicitly for brainiacs above all. But it's striking to notice the companies that don't put extreme cognitive abilities at the top of the list, or sometimes even on the list.

Exhibit A would be the company that corporate headhunters consistently rank number 1 as their hunting ground for business leaders, General Electric. CEO Jeff Immelt has been clear about what the company is looking for: someone who is externally focused, is a clear thinker, has imagination, is an inclusive leader, and is a confident expert. Those are behaviors, not traits, and an IQ of 130 is not required in order to exhibit them. Immelt's predecessor, Welch, used a different set of criteria that also was not cognitively focused. He was looking for four *E*'s: energy, ability to energize, edge (which means decisiveness, but he needed a word that started with *e*), and ability to execute. Again, those are behaviors, and they don't require special intelligence, memory, or more specific traits. It must be said that many GE leaders do seem awfully smart, but, then, those chess masters seem to have astonishing memories, when what they really have is a little different. So without testing, it's hard to know exactly what we're seeing. It's notable how many GE leaders—as distinct from those at McKinsey, Goldman, et al.—did not go to elite universities.

More generally, many top-performing companies have worked hard to develop hiring criteria and have come up with lists that clearly work but do not include standout general abilities. Southwest Airlines, the only airline in America to have made a profit every year for the past thirty-six years, is famous for seeking a blend of attitudes and personality traits—sense of humor, sense of mission, energy, confidence.

The message from these companies raises an important question: Even if superior intelligence and memory aren't the critical factors for success, are the traits these companies seek—team orientation, humor, confidence, and so on—reliably related to success across companies, and if so, are they innate traits that you either have or you don't? Research suggests that some personality dimensions do match up with success at certain types of work; yes, salespeople tend to be more extroverted, for example.

Logical next question: Are you stuck with the personality traits you have? Research going back decades suggests that personality dimensions don't vary much over the course of a person's life. But of course that doesn't necessarily limit a person's achievement; it may limit only the fields in which a person is most likely to excel. In addition, even within a given field, we know that some of the most successful people in business changed their personalities in significant ways. Former Treasury Secretary Robert Rubin, who spent most of his career at Goldman Sachs and became the firm's cochief, reports that in his early years at Goldman he was, essentially, a jerk. He admits that he was "short with people," "impersonal," "abrupt and peremptory," and frequently not nice to colleagues. None of this hindered his career as a successful arbitrageur; no one much cared how traders behaved as long as they delivered results. But then one day an older partner told Rubin he could possibly play a larger role in the firm if he changed his ways and actually started to care about the people he worked with. As Rubin recalls in his memoir, "I've often asked myself why this advice affected me so much." He speculates on reasons, but the bottom line is that it affected him deeply. He started listening to people better, understanding their problems, and valuing their views. He changed an important element of his personality. If he hadn't, it's unlikely he would have become one of the most respected and admired figures at Goldman and on Wall Street.

Psychologists might argue that people who do what Rubin did aren't changing their personalities, they're changing their behavior in order to override some part of their personalities. Fine; there's no need to quibble. What matters is that they were not constrained by particular traits.

At this point you can't help but wonder if there's anything at all (a) that makes a significant difference to whether you achieve extraordinary performance, and (b) that you can't do anything about. The answer is yes, of course there is. Most obvious are congenital physical and mental health problems, plus other diseases and disorders that may visit any of us at any time for reasons we still don't fully understand. Those constraints aside, and considering only people in general good health, the clearly innate limitations seem to be physical. Once you've matured physically, you can't do much about your height, and if you're five feet tall you're just never going to be an NFL lineman, while if you're seven feet tall you will not be an Olympic gymnast. Overall body size is also partly innate, so champion sumo wrestlers can probably never make themselves into elite marathoners. While you can develop your voice in all kinds of ways, the dimensions of your vocal cords impose limits; a tenor cannot make himself into a basso profundo.

That is all widely agreed upon. What's surprising is that when it comes to innate, unalterable limits on what healthy adults can achieve, anything beyond those physical constraints is in dispute. Clear evidence that such nonphysical constraints exist has not been found so far.

That fact is profoundly opposed to what most of us believe. We tend to think we are forever barred from all manner of successes because of what we were or were not born with. The range of cases in which that belief is true turns out to be a great deal narrower than most of us think. The roadblocks we face seem to be mostly imaginary.

This finding alone, however, is frustrating. We may have determined that there are hardly any immutable factors that prevent us from ever playing a work more difficult than "Chopsticks" on the piano, or from doing word problems in math, or from leading an organization larger than a softball team. But what we'd really like to know is not what does or doesn't stop us, but what makes some people go so much further than others. And what we have discovered so far is not what makes some people excel but rather what doesn't. Specifically:

• It isn't experience. Not only are we surrounded by highly experienced people who are nowhere near great at what they do, but we have also seen evidence that some people in a wide range of fields actually get worse after years of doing something.

• It isn't specific inborn abilities. We've seen extensive evidence that calls into question whether such abilities exist, and even if certain types of them might, they clearly do not determine excellence.

People who seem to possess abilities of this type do not necessarily achieve high performance, and we've seen many examples of people showing no evidence of such abilities who have produced extraordinary achievement.

• It isn't general abilities such as intelligence and memory. The research finds that in many fields the relation between intelligence and performance is weak or nonexistent; people with modest IQs sometimes perform outstandingly while people with high IQs sometimes don't get past mediocrity. Memory seems clearly to be acquired.

In short, we've nailed down what doesn't drive great performance. So what does?

Chapter Four

A Better Idea

An explanation of great performance
that makes sense

Growing up in Crawford, Mississippi (population: 636), Jerry Rice had to be talked into joining his high school's football team. The coach had reportedly heard that the young man was fast and persuaded him to try out. Rice played well and was named to the All-State team, but not so well that any big-name college would offer him a scholarship. Eventually Mississippi Valley State University in Itta Bena, Mississippi (population: 1,946), did offer him a football scholarship, and that's where he spent the next four years.

Rice was a big star at the little school, setting many NCAA records as a receiver. In his senior season he was named to every All-America team and was even a long-shot candidate for the Heisman Trophy (he didn't win). Again, however, he was not so extraordinary that NFL teams were fighting one another to get him. The problem was his speed; while he was fast by the standards of Crawford, and he was fast enough to be a college star, in the NFL his speed was nothing special. In the 1985 draft, fifteen teams passed him over before the San Francisco 49ers finally signed him.

As every football fan knows, Jerry Rice was the greatest receiver in NFL history, and some football authorities believe he may have been the greatest player at any position. His utter dominance is hard to believe in a league where the competition is so intense and conducted at such a high level. For example, the records he holds for total receptions, total touchdown receptions, and total receiving yards are greater than the second-place totals not by 5 percent or 10 percent, which would be impressive, but by about 50 percent.

It's always dangerous to suggest that any record will never be broken, but breaking Rice's records will be a particular challenge because he was an iron man. He played twenty seasons at a position that is notoriously perilous, and he played in almost every game of every season except one, 1997, when he was out for fourteen weeks because of an injury and returned sooner than his doctors advised. For some future player to perform at such an extremely high standard for so many years in a physically brutal game is obviously not impossible, but history suggests that it is unlikely.

What Made Rice So Good?

With regard to most players, that kind of question usually guarantees an argument among sports fans, but in Rice's case the answer is completely noncontroversial. Everyone in the football world seems to agree that Rice was the greatest because he worked harder in practice and in the off-season than anyone else.

In team workouts he was famous for his hustle; while many receivers will trot back to the quarterback after catching a pass, Rice would *sprint* to the end zone after each reception. He would typically continue practicing long after the rest of the team had gone home. Most remarkable were his six-days-a-week off-season workouts, which he conducted entirely on his own. Mornings were devoted to cardiovascular work, running a hilly five-mile trail; he would reportedly run ten forty-meter wind sprints up the steepest part. In the afternoons he did equally strenuous weight training. These workouts became legendary as the most demanding in the league, and other players would sometimes join Rice just to see what it was like. Some of them got sick before the day was over.

Occasionally someone would write to the 49ers' trainer asking for the details of Rice's workout, but the trainer never released the information out of fear that people would hurt themselves trying to duplicate it.

The lesson that's easiest to draw from Jerry Rice's story is that hard work makes all the difference. Yet we know—from research and from just looking around us—that hard work often doesn't lead to extraordinary performance. We also know that even after an excellent college career, Rice did not possess outstanding speed, a quality that coaches generally consider mandatory in a great receiver. So there must be something else lurking in Rice's story.

There is. Note several relevant points:

He spent very little time playing football.

Of all the work Rice did to make himself a great player, practically none of it was playing football games. His independent off-season workouts consisted of conditioning, and his team workouts were classroom study, reviewing of game films, conditioning, and lots of work with other players on specific plays. But the 49ers and eventually the other teams for which Rice played almost never ran full-contact scrimmages because they didn't want to risk injuring players. That means that of the total time Rice spent actually playing the game for which he became famous, nearly all of it was in the weekly games themselves.

How large a part of his football-related work was that? Let's estimate very conservatively that over the course of a year, Rice averaged 20 hours a week working on football; the work is demanding and even the most dedicated player can sustain only a limited amount. There is evidence that Rice probably averaged much more than that, but let's play it safe. That's about 1,000 hours a year, or 20,000 hours over his pro career. He played 303 career NFL games—the most ever by a wide receiver—and if we assume the offense had the ball half the time on average, that's about 150 hours of playing time as measured by the game clock; this may be overstated, since Rice wasn't on the field for every play. The conclusion we reach is that one of the greatest-ever football players devoted less than 1 percent of his football-related work to playing games.

Of course it's true that all NFL players devote most of their work-related time to nongame activities, and that fact is significant. These people, doing their work at its highest level and subject to continuous, unsparing evaluation, don't set up weekday football games for practice; they spend almost all their time on other activities, a fact that we should remember. In the case of Rice, one of the greatest players, the ratio was even more extreme.

He designed his practice to work on his specific needs.

Rice didn't need to do everything well, just certain things. He had to run precise patterns; he had to evade the defenders, sometimes two or three, who were assigned to cover him; he had to outjump them to catch the ball and outmuscle them when they tried to strip it away; then he had to outrun tacklers. So he focused his practice work on exactly those requirements. Not being the fastest receiver in the league turned out not to matter. He became famous for the precision of his patterns. His weight training gave him tremendous strength. His trail running gave him control so he could change directions suddenly without signaling his move. The uphill wind sprints game him explosive acceleration. Most of all, his endurance training—not something that a speed-focused athlete would normally concentrate on—gave him a giant advantage in the fourth quarter, when his opponents were tired and weak, and he seemed as fresh as he was in the first minute. Time and again, that's when he put the game away.

Rice and his coaches understood exactly what he needed in order to be dominant. They focused on those things and not on other goals that might have seemed generally desirable, like speed.

While supported by others, he did much of the work on his own.

The football season lasts less than half the year. A team sport obviously requires that the players work together a great deal, yet most of Rice's work was in the off-season. He had the important advice of coaches and trainers, but he did most of his football-related work by himself.

It wasn't fun.

There's nothing enjoyable about running to the point of exhaustion or lifting weights to the point of muscle failure. But these were centrally important activities.

He defied the conventional limits of age.

The average NFL player leaves the league in his twenties; playing at age thirty-five is an unusual achievement. The widely accepted view is that even if a player avoids injury, deterioration of the body is inevitable, and a player in his late thirties can no longer prevail when facing an opponent fifteen years younger. The few players who have remained starters into their forties have overwhelmingly been quarterbacks, who don't block and don't run much on most plays, or kickers and punters, who are in for only a few plays per game and are rarely even touched by the opponents. Wide receivers, who run like hell on most plays and frequently get crushed by tacklers, aren't supposed to last twenty seasons or play until age forty-two. None but Rice has ever done so.

The Crucial Finding

It's natural to question how much relevance a football star's career might have for the rest of us, and besides, it's just one person's story. From a scientific perspective it's an anecdote, not data. To see whether the apparent lessons of Rice's career might apply more broadly, con-

sider a critically important and highly rigorous scientific study conducted in the early nineties in a very different place, Berlin, and
examining a very different realm, music.

The object of the study was to figure out why some violinists are
better than others. The researchers went to the Music Academy of West
Berlin, as it was then known, a postsecondary school that turns out extremely good musicians, many of whom go on to careers with major
symphony orchestras or as solo performers. Professors were asked to
nominate the very best violinists, those with the potential for careers
as international soloists. The professors also nominated violinists who
were very good but not as good as the top group. In addition, the academy had a separate department with lower admission standards, the
students of which generally go on to become music teachers, and the
researchers recruited a group from this department as well. That made
three groups of test subjects—we'll call them good, better, and best—
which the researchers chose to be as similar as possible in age (all students were in their early twenties) and sex.

The researchers then collected lots of biographical data about all the
subjects—the age at which they started studying music, the teachers
they had, the competitions they had entered, and much else. The data
confirmed the judgments of the music professors: The best violinists
had been more successful in competitions than the better ones, who had
been more successful than the good ones. The subjects were asked to
estimate how many hours a week they practiced for each year since
they started. They were given a long list of activities, music-related and
non-music-related, and asked how much time they had spent on each
one in the most recent typical week; they were also asked to rate how
relevant each activity was to making them better violinists, how effortful it was, and how enjoyable it was. They were asked a great deal more,
including how they had spent the previous day, minute by minute, and
they were asked to fill out a detailed diary for a week. Because diary

reports aren't always accurate, the researchers cross-checked them in various ways and conducted extensive interviews with the subjects afterward to confirm the validity of the numbers.

The result was a vast trove of data. A layman looking at it all would simply conclude that the lives and behaviors of these violinists had been analyzed thirteen ways from Sunday. But as it happened, the results that emerged from all this analysis were particularly clear and strong.

By many measures, all three groups of violinists were about the same. They all started studying the violin at around age eight and decided to become musicians at around age fifteen, with no statistically significant differences among the groups. By the time of the study, every subject had been studying the violin for at least a decade.

Perhaps most striking, all three groups were spending the same total amount of time on music-related activities—lessons, practice, classes, and so on—about fifty-one hours a week. The researchers found no statistically significant differences among the groups on this measure. That is, all three groups were getting up every morning and putting in the hours, throwing themselves at their chosen career in a fairly committed way with a demanding workweek equal to what a great many people clock in a wide range of fields.

The violinists were quite certain which activity was most important for making them better: It was practicing by themselves. When asked to rate the relevance of twelve music-related activities and ten non-music-related activities (such as household chores, shopping, leisure) to their progress, solitary practice was number one with a bullet.

They all knew it, but they didn't all do it. Though the violinists understood the importance of practice alone, the amount of time the various groups actually spent practicing alone differed dramatically. The two top groups, the best and better violinists, practiced by themselves about twenty-four hours a week on average. The third group, the good violinists, practiced by themselves only nine hours a week.

This finding becomes even richer with meaning when we consider other aspects of practice. Just as the violinists were sure that it's the most important activity, they were also quite clear that it's hard and it isn't much fun. When they rated activities by effort required, solo practice ranked way harder than playing music for fun, alone or with others, and harder than even the most effortful everyday activity, child care. As for pleasure, practice ranked far below playing for fun and even below formal group performance, which you might reasonably guess would be the most stressful and least fun activity.

Practice is so hard that doing a lot of it requires people to arrange their lives in particular ways. The two top groups of violinists did most of their practicing in the late morning or early afternoon, when they were still fairly fresh. By contrast, violinists in the third group practiced mostly in the late afternoon, when they were more likely to be tired. The two top groups differed from the third group in another way: They slept more. They not only slept more at night, they also took far more afternoon naps. All that practicing seems to demand a lot of recovery.

Solo practice is unusual among music-related activities in that it's largely within the individual's control. Most other activities—taking lessons, attending classes, giving performances—require other people's involvement and are therefore constrained. But with 168 hours in a week, a person can practice by himself or herself just about without limit. In fact, no one in the study came anywhere near spending every available hour on practice.

So all the violinists understood that practicing by themselves was the most important thing they could do to get better. Though they didn't consider it easy or fun, they all had virtually unlimited time in which to do it. On those dimensions, they were all the same. The difference was that some chose to practice more, and those violinists were a great deal better.

The advantage of practice was cumulative. You may have noticed that at the time of the study, the best and better violinists were practicing about the same amount, twenty-four hours a week. While this was enormously more practice than the merely good violinists were doing, the researchers didn't find a significant difference in practice time between the two top groups. That lack of difference would seem to pose a problem. If more practice equals better performance, then why isn't the best group practicing any more than the middle group?

The answer lies in the students' histories. All the research subjects were asked to estimate their weekly practice hours for each year of their violin-playing lives, enabling the researchers to calculate cumulative lifetime totals. The results were extraordinarily clear. By age eighteen, the violinists in the first group had accumulated 7,410 hours of lifetime practice on average, versus 5,301 hours for violinists in the second group and 3,420 hours for those in the third group. All the differences were statistically significant.

Again, the implications are even stronger than they may first appear. Yes, more total practice is very powerfully associated with better performance. But now imagine the situation of a violinist in the third group who decides at age eighteen that he wants to become an international soloist, the next Itzhak Perlman or Joshua Bell. The hard reality is that the best violinists of his age, the ones he'll have to match or beat, have already racked up more than twice as much practice time as he has. If he wants to catch up, he'll have to practice far more than they do, even though he's currently practicing far less (nine hours a week versus twenty-four). So he'll have to multiply his practice time by a huge factor if he wants to catch up before he's an old man, and he'll have to make this all-consuming commitment at just the point in life when a person is expected to take on adult responsibilities and start becoming financially independent. In short, it may be possible in theory for our young man or woman to vault into the world of elite violin soloists, but as a practical matter it will be nearly impossible. The issues implicit in his situation turn out to be highly significant for individuals and organizations generally.

This study was extraordinarily persuasive in answering the question of why some violinists are so much better than others. It was part of a landmark paper on the larger question of why certain people in any field—business, sports, music, science, arts—were extremely good while most people were not. The lead author of that paper—"The Role of Deliberate Practice in the Acquisition of Expert Performance"—was Anders Ericsson, the man who fifteen years earlier had helped conduct the experiment with the screaming undergraduate who could remember eighty-two random digits. The implications of that research had never left Ericsson's mind. Now, in this new paper, he and his coauthors, Ralf Th. Krampe and Clemens Tesch-Römer of the Max Planck Institute for Human Development and Education, were proposing a new theoretical framework for understanding why some people are so remarkably good at what they do.

They proposed this new framework because the existing one, which relied heavily on the concept of innate talent, was so clearly unsatisfactory. We've already seen many of the problems with it, such as the numerous cases of great performers who showed no evidence of precocity or natural gifts. In addition to these problems, Ericsson and his coauthors had noticed another theme that emerged in research on top-level performers: No matter who they were, or what explanation of their performance was being advanced, it always took them many years to become excellent, and if a person achieves elite status only after many years of toil, assigning the principal role in that success to innate gifts becomes problematic, to say the least.

The phenomenon seems nearly universal. In a famous study of chess players, Nobel Prize winner Herbert Simon and William Chase (Ericsson's coauthor on the memory study) proposed "the ten-year rule," based on their observation that no one seemed to reach the top ranks of chess players without a decade or so of intensive study, and some required much more time. Even Bobby Fischer was not an exception; when he became a grand master at age sixteen, he had been studying chess intensively for nine years. Subsequent research in a wide range of fields has substantiated the ten-year rule everywhere the researchers have looked. In math, science, musical composition, swimming, X-ray diagnosis, tennis, literature—no one, not even the most "talented" performers, became great without at least ten years of very hard preparation. If talent means that success is easy or rapid, as most people seem to believe, then something is obviously wrong with a talent-based explanation of high achievement.

As researchers went further down this road, they noticed something else: Many scientists and authors produce their greatest work only after twenty or more years of devoted effort, which means that in year nineteen they are still getting better. That fact posed additional problems for the talent-based view of exceptional achievement. Francis Galton was absolutely convinced that every person is born with various limits that he simply cannot get past: "His maximum performance becomes a rigidly determinate quantity." Those limits apply to every kind of endeavor, physical or mental. A person bumps up against his or her limits fairly early in life, Galton believed, and after that, "unless he is incurably blinded by self-conceit, he learns precisely of what performance he is capable, and what other enterprises lie beyond his compass." At that sobering moment, Galton said, the wise person literally gives up trying to do more. "He is no longer tormented into hopeless efforts by the fallacious promptings of overweening vanity. . . ." He discards the foolish notion that he can ever do better, makes peace with the idea that he's as good as he'll ever be, and "finds true moral repose in an honest conviction that he is engaged in as much good work as his nature has rendered him capable of performing." At least Galton made it sound noble.

Yet a hundred years later, abundant evidence showed clearly that people can keep getting better long after they should have reached their "rigidly determinate" natural limits. The examples were not just great writers, artists, businesspeople, inventors, and other eminences producing their best work three or four decades into their careers. By the late nineteenth century, scientific research was showing repeatedly that ordinary people in various lines of work could keep getting better even after their performance had apparently plateaued. Typists, telegraph operators, typesetters—highly experienced workers in all these jobs, whose performance hadn't improved in years, suddenly got markedly better when they were offered incentives or given new kinds of training. This evidence was obviously a big problem for the you've-got-it-or-you-don't view of achievement.

Summing up the extensive evidence, Ericsson and his coauthors observed that "the search for stable heritable characteristics that could predict or at least account for the superior performance of eminent individuals has been surprisingly unsuccessful." Yet at the time of their article, the talent-based view of high achievement was still the explanation most widely favored. Why? The authors offered a simple reason: "The conviction in the importance of talent appears to be based on the insufficiency of alternative hypotheses to explain the exceptional nature of expert performers."

That is, no one had a better idea. So here was their better idea.

It could be put very simply: What the authors called "deliberate practice" makes all the difference. Or as they stated it with stark clarity in their scholarly paper, "the differences between expert performers and normal adults reflect a life-long period of deliberate effort to improve performance in a specific domain."

This position was highly significant for two reasons. First, it explicitly rejected the you've-got-it-or-you-don't view. It explained high achievement without the concept of talent playing any role. The authors accepted that the great performers in any field really are qualitatively different from the rest of us but disputed the common view of where those differences come from. As they stated, "we deny that these differences are immutable, that is, due to innate talent." So here was a fundamentally new view of why some people are so extremely good at what they do.

The second reason why Ericsson et al.'s new framework was significant is that it resolved the huge contradiction in the body of scholarly research on performance and high achievement as well as in our everyday experience. On the one hand, we see everywhere that years of hard work do not make most people great at what they do. If all we did was open our eyes and look around, we would probably agree with Galton: The vast majority of people we work with, or play golf with, or play Doom with, got better for a while and then leveled off, having apparently reached the limit of their abilities; years of further work have not made them any better. On the other hand, we see repeatedly that the people who have achieved the most are the ones who have worked the hardest. How can both sets of observations be true?

The framework advanced by Ericsson and his colleagues goes to the heart of this contradiction. The problem, they observed, is that "the current definition of practice is vague." Their framework is not based on a simplistic "practice makes perfect" observation. Rather, it is based on their highly specific concept of "deliberate practice."

Precisely what this means turns out to be critically important. It does not mean what most people think it does. An understanding of it illuminates the path to high achievement in any field, not just by individuals but also by teams and organizations. And by the way, it shows, among many other things, that Jerry Rice knew exactly what he was doing.

Chapter Five

What Deliberate Practice Is and Isn't

*For starters, it isn't what most of us do
when we're "practicing."*

We all know what practice is. I do it all the time. Odds are good that you do it in a similar general way, regardless of what you're practicing. When I practice golf, I go to the driving range and get two big buckets of balls. I pick my spot, put down my bag of clubs, and tip over one of the buckets. I read somewhere that you should warm up with short irons, so I take out an 8- or 9-iron and start hitting. I also read somewhere that you should always have a target, so I pick one of the fake "greens" out on the range and aim for it, though I'm not really sure how far away it is. As I work through the short irons, middle irons, long irons, and driver, I hit quite a few bad shots. My usual reaction is to hit another ball as quickly as possible in hopes that it will be a decent shot, and then I can forget about the bad one.

Occasionally I realize that I should stop to think about why the shot was bad. There seem to be about five thousand things you can do wrong when hitting a golf ball, so I pick one of them and work on it a bit, convincing myself that I can sense improvement, until I hit another bad one, at which point I figure I should probably also work on another one of the five thousand things. Not long thereafter the two buckets of balls are gone and I head back to the clubhouse, very much looking forward to playing an actual game of golf, and feeling virtuous for having practiced.

But in truth I have no justification for feeling virtuous. Whatever it was I was doing out on the range, and regardless of whether I call it practice, it hasn't accomplished a thing.

The Elements

The concept of deliberate practice, advanced by Anders Ericsson and his colleagues and since investigated by many other researchers, is quite specific. It isn't work and isn't play, but is something entirely unto itself. We commonly use the term "practice" when talking about two domains, sports and music, but that habit can lead us astray. As already suggested, what we think of as practice frequently isn't what the researchers mean by deliberate practice. Just as important, our habitual use of the term in sports and music may stop us from thinking of how deliberate practice can be applied in other domains, such as business or science, in which we almost never think about practicing. Examples from sports and music are highly instructional because they're familiar, but I'll explain in chapters 7, 8, and 9 how the same principles can be much more widely applied. Since this activity is the essence of great performance, we have much to gain by banishing preconceptions and opening our minds to what it really is.

Deliberate practice is characterized by several elements, each worth examining. It is activity designed specifically to improve performance, often with a teacher's help; it can be repeated a lot; feedback on results is continuously available; it's highly demanding mentally, whether the activity is purely intellectual, such as chess or business-related activities, or heavily physical, such as sports; and it isn't much fun.

Let's consider each of those attributes of deliberate practice and what it implies.

It's designed specifically to improve performance.

The key word in this attribute is *designed*. In the example of my pathetic routine on the driving range, I was designing my own practice activity, even though it's clear that I'm completely unqualified to do so. The mechanics of hitting golf balls have been studied for decades and are extremely well understood by those who have made it their profession, but I have virtually none of their knowledge. It's the same in almost every field: Decades or centuries of study have produced a body of knowledge about how performance is developed and improved, and full-time teachers generally possess that knowledge. At least in the early going, therefore, and sometimes long after, it's almost always necessary for a teacher to design the activity best suited to improve an individual's performance. In some fields, especially intellectual ones such as the arts, science, and business, people may eventually become skilled enough to design their own practice. But anyone who thinks they've outgrown the benefits of a teacher's help should at least question that view. There's a reason why the world's best golfers still go to teachers.

One of those reasons goes beyond the teacher's knowledge. It's his or her ability to see you in ways that you cannot see yourself. In sports the observation is literal; I cannot see myself hitting the golf ball and would benefit greatly from someone else's perspective. In other fields the observation may be metaphorical. A chess teacher is looking at the same boards as the student but can see that the student is consistently overlooking an important threat. A business coach is looking at the same situations as a manager but can see, for example, that the manager systematically fails to communicate his intentions clearly.

It's apparent why becoming significantly good at almost anything is extremely difficult without the help of a teacher or coach, at least in the early going. Without a clear, unbiased view of the subject's performance, choosing the best practice activity will be impossible; for reasons that may be simply physical (as in sports) or deeply psychological, very few of us can make a clear, honest assessment of our own performance. Even if we could, we could not design the best practice activity for that moment in our development—the type of practice that would put us on the road to achieving at the highest levels—unless we had extensive knowledge of the latest and best methods for developing people in our chosen field. Most of us don't have that knowledge.

While the best methods of development are constantly changing, they're always built around a central principle: They're meant to stretch the individual beyond his or her current abilities. That may sound obvious, but most of us don't do it in the activities we think of as practice. At the driving range or at the piano, most of us, as adults, are just doing what we've done before and hoping to maintain the level of performance that we probably reached long ago.

By contrast, deliberate practice requires that one identify certain sharply defined elements of performance that need to be improved, and then work intently on them. Examples are everywhere. The great soprano Joan Sutherland devoted countless hours to practicing her trill—and not just the basic trill, but the many different types (whole-tone, semitone, baroque). Tiger Woods has been seen to drop golf balls into a sand trap and step on them, then practice shots from that near-impossible lie. The great performers isolate remarkably specific aspects of what they do and focus on just those things until they are improved; then it's on to the next aspect.

Choosing these aspects of performance is itself an important skill. Noel Tichy, a professor at the University of Michigan business school and former chief of General Electric's famous Crotonville management development center, illustrates the point by drawing three concentric circles. He labels the inner circle "comfort zone," the middle one "learning zone," and the outer one "panic zone." Only by choosing activities in the learning zone can one make progress. That's the location of skills and abilities that are just out of reach. We can never make progress in the comfort zone because those are the activities we can already do easily, while panic-zone activities are so hard that we don't even know how to approach them.

Identifying the learning zone, which is not simple, and then forcing oneself to stay continually in it as it changes, which is even harder— these are the first and most important characteristics of deliberate practice.

It can be repeated a lot.

High repetition is the most important difference between deliberate practice of a task and performing the task for real, when it counts. Tiger Woods may face that buried lie in the sand only two or three times in a season, and if those were his only opportunities to work on hitting that shot, he certainly wouldn't be able to hit it very well.

Repeating a specific activity over and over is what most of us mean by practice, yet for most of us it isn't especially effective. After all, I was repeating something—hitting golf balls—on the driving range. Two points distinguish deliberate practice from what most of us actually do. One is the choice of a properly demanding activity in the learning zone, as discussed. My golf practice certainly failed on that criterion, since I wasn't focused on doing anything in particular. The other is the amount of repetition. Top performers repeat their practice activities to stultifying extent. Ted Williams, baseball's greatest hitter, would practice hitting until his hands bled. Pete Maravich, whose college basketball records still stand after more than thirty years, would go to the gym when it opened in the morning and shoot baskets until it closed at night. An extreme and instructive example is the golfer Moe Norman, who played from the 1950s to the 1970s and never amounted to much on the pro tour because, for reasons of his own, he was never very interested in winning tournaments. He was just interested in hitting golf balls consistently well, and at this he may have been the greatest ever. Shot after shot was straight and just like the one before it. His practice routine from age sixteen to age thirty-two involved hitting eight hundred balls a day, five days a week. He was (perhaps obviously) obsessive about this and claimed to have kept count of all the practice balls he ever hit; by the mid-1990s he was up to four million. Top-level pro golf requires much more than just hitting straight shots, but at this particular skill, mind-boggling repetition produced amazing ability.

More generally, the most effective deliberate practice activities are those that can be repeated at high volume.

Feedback on results is continuously available.

Steve Kerr, former chief learning officer of Goldman Sachs and a highly respected researcher on leadership development, says that practicing without feedback is like bowling through a curtain that hangs down to knee level. You can work on technique all you like, but if you can't see the effects, two things will happen: You won't get any better, and you'll stop caring.

Getting feedback on most practice activities is easy. Lift the curtain and a bowler knows immediately how he did; in sports generally, seeing the results of practice is no problem. Aspiring chess masters practice by studying chess games played by the greatest players; at each position, the student chooses a move and then gets feedback by seeing what the champion did. Difficulties arise when the results require interpretation. You may believe you played that bar of the Brahms Violin Concerto perfectly, but can you really trust your own judgment? Or you may think that your rehearsal of a job interview was flawless, but your opinion isn't what counts. These are situations in which a teacher, coach, or mentor is vital for providing crucial feedback.

It's highly demanding mentally.

Deliberate practice is above all an effort of focus and concentration. That is what makes it "deliberate," as distinct from the mindless playing of scales or hitting of tennis balls that most people engage in. Continually seeking exactly those elements of performance that are unsatisfactory and then trying one's hardest to make them better places enormous strains on anyone's mental abilities.

The work is so great that it seems no one can sustain it for very long. A finding that is remarkably consistent across disciplines is that four or five hours a day seems to be the upper limit of deliberate practice, and this is frequently accomplished in sessions lasting no more than an hour to ninety minutes. The best violinists in the Berlin study, for example, practiced about three and a half hours a day, typically in two or three sessions. Many other top-level musicians report four or five hours as their upper limit. Chess champions typically report the same amount of practice. Even elite athletes say the factor that limits their practice time is their ability to sustain concentration.

Nathan Milstein, one of the twentieth century's greatest violinists, was a student of the famous teacher Leopold Auer (the one who pronounced Tchaikovsky's Violin Concerto unplayable, though he later became a big fan of it). As the story goes, Milstein asked Auer if he was practicing enough. Auer responded, "Practice with your fingers and you need all day. Practice with your mind and you will do as much in one and a half hours."

What Auer didn't add is that it's a good thing one and a half hours are enough, because if you're practicing with your mind, you couldn't possibly keep it up all day.

It isn't much fun.

This follows inescapably from the other characteristics of deliberate practice, which could be described as a recipe for not having fun. Doing things we know how to do well is enjoyable, and that's exactly the opposite of what deliberate practice demands. Instead of doing what we're good at, we insistently seek out what we're not good at. Then we identify the painful, difficult activities that will make us better and do those things over and over. After each repetition, we force ourselves to see— or get others to tell us—exactly what still isn't right so we can repeat the most painful and difficult parts of what we've just done. We continue that process until we're mentally exhausted.

Ericsson and his colleagues stated it clearly in their article: Deliberate practice "is not inherently enjoyable."

If it seems a bit depressing that the most important thing you can do to improve performance is no fun, take consolation in this fact: It must be so. If the activities that lead to greatness were easy and fun, then everyone would do them and they would not distinguish the best from the rest. The reality that deliberate practice is hard can even be seen as good news. It means that most people won't do it. So your willingness to do it will distinguish you all the more.

Lessons from Chris Rock

That is a brief initial description of deliberate practice, the series of activities that seems to explain great performance most persuasively. If you work in one of the fields in which the concept of practice is most deeply entrenched—sports and music—you're probably thinking that Ericsson and his colleagues have explained and elaborated ideas that many people in your world have understood for a long time. But if you're among the far more numerous people who make a living in business-related fields, you're probably thinking: This is absolutely nothing like work!

In fact, life at most companies seems almost intended to defeat all the principles of deliberate practice.

Most fundamentally, what we generally do at work is directly opposed to the first principle: It isn't designed by anyone to make us better at anything. Usually it isn't designed at all; we're just given an objective that's necessary to meeting the employer's goals and are expected to get on with it. From the limited, short-term perspective of many employers, this is completely justified. We weren't hired so we could spend time improving our own abilities; we were hired to produce results.

As for the second principle, the activities that would make us better are usually not highly repeatable. When we face new or unusual challenges—a competitor's innovation, a shift in customer attitudes—we typically find little past experience to guide us because we've had so few chances to deal with those situations. We're golfers encountering the buried-lie sand shot two or three times a year, but we haven't practiced it two hundred times. Even in jobs where we do the same few things—negotiating with suppliers, administering benefits—we face few (if any) incentives to get better at them by exceeding our limits and discovering what we can't do well. On the contrary, while deliberate practice demands that we push ourselves to the point where we break down and then develop a solution, in our business lives the cost of mistakes is often high. Every incentive urges us to stick with what's safe and reliable.

Feedback? At most companies this is a travesty, consisting of an annual performance review dreaded by the person delivering it and the one receiving it. Even if it's well done, it cannot be very effective. Telling someone what he did well or poorly on a task he completed eleven months ago is just not helpful.

You could say that work, like deliberate practice, is often mentally demanding and tiring. But that's typically not because of the intense focus and concentration involved. Rather, it's more often a result of long hours cranking out what we already know how to do. And if we're exhausted from that, the prospect of spending additional hours on genuine deliberate practice activities seems too miserable to contemplate. Similarly, work is often not fun. But again, that's not because we're trying to push beyond the edge of our abilities. It's because getting anything accomplished in the real world is a grind.

If that's life in most companies, then the opportunities for achieving

advantage by adopting the principles of great performance, individually and organizationally, would seem to be huge. In fact they are, and
in later chapters we'll look in detail at how that can be done. But first
it's helpful to consider a bit more deeply just what deliberate practice
is. Indeed, what's especially surprising about the cluelessness of most
organizations with regard to deliberate practice is that the principles
are not counterintuitive or hard to grasp. On the contrary, once we hear
them enunciated, we start seeing them—and their effectiveness—in
many domains.

Consider, as one example, how the comedian Chris Rock prepared
for a high-profile, high-stakes performance he was to give on New Year's
Eve before an audience of twenty thousand at Madison Square Garden.
A newspaper article sets up the story as follows:

> Because he has been on top of the comic heap so long, it is easy to
> assume that Mr. Rock can make that whole big room shake with the
> same convulsive laughter because he was born that way. Like Tiger
> Woods, Bill Clinton or Tom Brady, he seems genetically predisposed
> to do precisely what he does.

It sounds like the article will be a classic example of the divine-spark
theory, but in fact the article's point is exactly the opposite. This is
some of its remarkable description of how Chris Rock prepared for his
appearance:

> The least surprised person when that first laugh starts and then
> moves in a wave all the way up to the cheap seats will be Mr. Rock.
> For many months he has been piecing together his act in clubs in
> New Jersey, New York, Florida and Las Vegas. Comedy bit by comedy
> bit, he has built two hours of material one minute at a time, culling
> the belly laughs from the bombs. . . .
> For him the 18 warm-up shows he did at the Stress Factory in New

Brunswick, N.J., preparing for the tour are more important than his three Emmys.

"He knows that they are going to give him that first laugh because of who he is," said Vinnie Brand, the owner of the Stress Factory. "But he came out here and worked his material, over and over, cutting and trimming, until by the last show you could not believe what he had put together. He still has that hunger to be a great stand-up comedian, no matter what his name is."

Here we see all the elements of deliberate practice. Rock designed all those small-club appearances for the sole purpose of making himself better; because he already performs at a very high level, he's completely qualified to design his own practice. The high repetition in the process is particularly striking—appearance after appearance, working the material "over and over." Feedback happens to be no problem in Rock's profession; the reaction of the audience—the only thing that counts—is immediate and continuous (and brutally honest). It's clear that Rock must be focusing intensely on the process and that it can't be much fun, especially when new material doesn't work, as must happen often. The result is Rock's vast success; as the article put it, "if he is not the funniest man alive, then the other guy is doing a good job of hiding."

A particularly dramatic illustration of deliberate practice is useful because it highlights the principles so clearly. It's the story of the Polgar sisters.

Laszlo Polgar, a Hungarian educational psychologist, formed the view in the 1960s that great performers are made, not born. His research persuaded him that the greatest performers had all been made to focus and work on their field of eventual achievement from an early age, and he believed he understood the process well enough that he could make it happen himself. He wrote a book about how to do it (English translation of the title: *Bring Up Genius!*) and publicly asked for a woman who would marry him, have children with him, and help him conduct the experiment. Amazingly enough, he found such a woman, a Hungarian-speaking schoolteacher in the Ukraine named Klara.

Laszlo and Klara soon had a daughter, Susan, and when Susan turned four the experiment began. Exactly why Laszlo decided to turn Susan into a chess player is not clear. By some accounts it was because progress in chess is apparent and easy to measure from the beginning. By other accounts it was because chess is heavily male-dominated, and the prevailing view was that women were simply incapable of competing at the highest level—so this would be the ideal realm in which Laszlo could prove his theory.

Laszlo and Klara devoted their lives to teaching Susan chess, and when two more daughters followed—Sophia and Judit—they were put into the program as well. All three daughters were homeschooled—the parents quit their jobs to devote themselves to the work—and the schooling consisted largely of chess instruction. The family accumulated a library of ten thousand chess books. A giant pre-computer-age filing system of index cards cataloged previous games and potential opponents. The daughters learned other subjects as well; the Hungarian authorities insisted that they all pass regular exams in school subjects, and all three daughters spoke several languages. But chess was the main thing—hours and hours of it every day.

The results: At age seventeen, Susan became the first woman to qualify for what was then called the Men's World Championship (though she qualified, the World Chess Federation wouldn't let her compete). When Susan was nineteen, Sophia fourteen, and Judit twelve, they competed as a team in the Women's Olympiad and scored Hungary's first-ever victory against the Soviets, becoming national heroes. At age twenty-one, Susan became the first woman ever to be named a grand master, the highest rank in world chess. Soon thereafter, Judit became a grand master at age fifteen, the youngest person of either sex ever to win that designation, beating Bobby Fischer's previous record by a few months. As of this writing Judit is the world's number 1 woman player, and for years she ranked consistently in the top ten of all players worldwide.

The Polgars' story is exceptionally useful because it illustrates the principles of deliberate practice through what the sisters achieved as well as through what they did not. Overall, of course, their tremendous success would seem to validate emphatically what their father believed. There was no reason to suppose that Laszlo or Klara passed on any innate chess ability to their daughters; Laszlo was only a mediocre player, and Klara had demonstrated no chess ability at all. The children's success would seem to have resulted only from their years of intensive work, which met the definition of deliberate practice in every particular.

At the same time, it must be noted that the daughters did not achieve equal levels of success, and none of them reached the very highest level, the world championship. But these facts are also consistent with the principles of deliberate practice. The middle sister, Sophia, did not reach the heights scaled by her two sisters (though she did become the sixth-ranked woman in the world), and everyone seems to agree that she was the least committed. A lengthy magazine profile of the sisters quoted chess champion Josh Waitzkin as saying Sophia "was a brilliant speed player, sharp as a tack. But she didn't work as hard as the others." Susan said that Sophia "was lazy." And even Sophia agreed: "I could give up easier than Judit. I never worked as hard as she did." Similarly, everyone seems to agree that Judit, who rose highest, worked hardest at practice. It would also stand to reason that by the time Judit, the youngest, came along, Laszlo had refined his methods of practice design.

As for the fact that none of the sisters became a world champion, it may be hazardous to speculate on why things work out as they do in the rarefied air of the very highest levels. But it's certainly worth noting that when they were in their twenties, when future champions are typically still fighting for their shot at the top, all three sisters decided there was more to life than chess. (As Sophia was quoted as saying: "It's not that chess was too much for me; it was too little.") They got married, had kids, gave time to their families, and eased up on the unrelenting chess-focused work that had filled their lives until then.

Their own stories have convinced them that their father was right. Susan said, "My father believes that innate talent is nothing, that [success] is 99 percent hard work. I agree with him." More specifically, the story of the Polgars illustrates how the principles of deliberate practice, when carried to an extraordinary level, produce extraordinary achievement.

What We Need to Know Next

It's easy to find more familiar stories that reinforce the validity of the deliberate practice framework. We can quickly see, for example, that Jerry Rice was a near-perfect example of the principles through what he did, and the intensity and focus with which he did it. We see that the story of Tiger Woods's development, described in chapter 2, conforms exactly to these principles. They are exemplified in the stories of almost every other top-level athlete, as well as in the lives of eminent musicians and many others. In particular, there are countless stories of people who not only seemed to lack any natural advantage in a field where they eventually excelled but were clearly disadvantaged—yet through these principles overcame the obstacles. One thinks of Wilma Rudolph, hobbled by polio as a child, who won three Olympic gold medals in track and field. Or the lisping Winston Churchill, who became one of the twentieth century's greatest orators by practicing his many speeches intensively and with great precision over a period of many years.

With the deliberate practice framework in mind, examples are everywhere. But questions immediately arise. The most pressing:

Is that all there is?

Does deliberate practice fully explain high achievement? Will someone who does twice as much of it as someone else be twice as successful? The answer to these questions is clearly no. Deliberate practice does not fully explain achievement—real life is too complicated for that. Most obviously, we're all affected by luck; time and chance happeneth to us all, as it says in Ecclesiastes. While it has often been observed that those who work the hardest seem to be the luckiest, the fact remains that if a bridge collapses while you're driving over it, nothing else matters. Less dramatically but much more significantly, a person's circumstances, especially in childhood, can powerfully affect his or her opportunities to engage in deliberate practice. We may say that Tiger Woods is a textbook illustration of the deliberate practice principles, but we could also say that he was breathtakingly lucky to be introduced to them. In this sense, it's perfectly fair to say that the real reason you'll never be Tiger Woods is that your father wasn't Earl Woods. In chapter 10 we'll look more closely at the importance of the supporting environment, much of which may be outside a person's control, especially in youth.

Beyond simple luck, we know that physical changes are inevitable over time. It turns out that deliberate practice can extend one's ability to perform at high levels far longer than most people believe, as we shall see in chapter 10. But ultimately we're all mortal, and our faculties decline. This fact may be more significant than it seems. A person's total lifetime hours of deliberate practice can never decline, so if that were the only factor that determined performance, no one would ever get worse at anything they've learned. Since everyone does get worse eventually, even if only at a very advanced age, then it must be possible for factors outside our control to affect our performance. We'll look into this more deeply later.

In addition, even though performance seems to improve with

increased deliberate practice in a wide range of research studies, it must also be true that the relationship cannot be simple and direct in every case. That is, there must be qualitative differences between my practice and yours. In many cases these will arise from the varying quality of teachers, coaches, and mentors. Practice is designed, so it can be designed well or badly.

Regardless of how well it's designed, another important variable is how much effort a person puts into it. We've all engaged in deliberate practice at something—a musical instrument, a sport, or something else—so we all understand Leopold Auer's remark about practicing with the mind. Some days we were sharp, focused, and working hard; other days we were tired, distracted, and going through the motions. Measuring the intensity of practice may be difficult, but it's clearly significant. A study of singers found that when amateurs took a voice lesson, they experienced it as an enjoyable release of tension, but when professionals took a lesson, they experienced it as an intense, difficult effort. Seen from the outside, they were doing the same thing, but on the inside they were doing completely different things, and that's what mattered.

Comparing hours of practice by large numbers of people reveals important trends, but comparing hours put in by specific people may not tell us much if we don't also know the intensity of practice. Which leads to a related question . . .

What determines who does it?

Considering that deliberate practice is so demanding and in itself unrewarding, and that high achievement demands thousands of hours of it over a period of many years, why do some people put themselves through it while most do not? If the road to extraordinary performance is apparent, then why do so few people choose to follow it? This turns out to be a very deep question, so deep that we devote an entire chapter to it (chapter 11). For the moment we note that merely raising the question introduces another significant issue . . .

Could the explanation possibly be genetic?

The whole notion of deliberate practice has for many people created the notion of a nature-versus-nurture battle, with practice advocates pitted against proponents of the divine-spark hypothesis. But it's important to note that advocates of the deliberate practice framework have never excluded the possibility of a genetic role in high-level performance. Their stance has been that they have not yet seen the evidence supporting it. Certainly if we're looking for specific DNA components that make someone an exceptional oboist or fighter pilot or salesperson—or, to put the same idea another way, if we're seeking specific DNA that limits a particular person's ability to excel in these fields—then the search has come up dry so far. But practice proponents do not dispute the possibility that genes could play a role in a person's willingness to put himself or herself through the extremely rigorous demands of becoming an exceptional performer.

Some people, especially those who favor explanations based on innate talents, just don't like that possibility, even though it's genetically based. They call it "the drudge theory." For now all we can say is that it's a hypothesis that has not been tested, let alone proved or disproved. We may well gain new insight into it as DNA research gallops forward. At the same time, that research is revealing many ways in which DNA and the environment interact from the moment of conception all the way through life, and suggesting increasingly that the concept of strict nature-versus-nurture conflict is unhelpful in understanding how people actually develop. This also is part of what we'll consider in chapter 11, after we've looked more closely into how deliberate practice works.

What is all that practice doing?

While it's clear that extensive deliberate practice will make someone a superior surgeon or billiard player or public speaker, it's natural to wonder if the effect can be understood in some general way. Beyond simply making a person better at the specific task they're practicing, is it doing something that applies across cases? The answer is yes, and it's worth identifying because it's the opposite of what most people think.

If you're a golf fan, you may have seen videotape of Tiger Woods in a particular situation that has occurred a few times in his career. He's in a tournament, standing over the ball, about to hit his shot. At some moment after he has begun his swing but before he has hit the ball, a major distraction happens—a fan yells, someone moves sharply, the crowd roars elsewhere on the course. Woods stops himself in midswing, steps back from the ball, recomposes himself, and then steps forward and hits the shot.

Ordinary golfers respond with awe when they see this happen because they know what they'd do in the same circumstance: Unable to stop their swing once they'd started it, they would carry through and hit a terrible shot or maybe miss the ball completely.

Why is this significant? Frequently when we see great performers doing what they do, it strikes us that they've practiced for so long, and done it so many times, they can just do it automatically. But in fact, what they have achieved is the ability to avoid doing it automatically.

When we learn to do anything new—how to drive, for example—we go through three stages. The first stage demands a lot of attention as we try out the controls, learn the rules of driving, and so on. In the second stage we begin to coordinate our knowledge, linking movements together and more fluidly combining our actions with our knowledge of the car, the situation, and the rules. In the third stage we drive the car with barely a thought. It's automatic. And with that our improvement at driving slows dramatically, eventually stopping completely.

For most of the things we do, including driving, that's not a problem. We don't need to be great at such things, just good enough to carry on with our lives. That category of activities includes golf for most people who play the game. They don't need to earn a living at it; they just want to be able to have fun with it. Not having to devote much thought to such activities is a blessing, since it frees our minds to focus on other matters that we consider more important. But it does mean that our brains have pretty much checked out when we're doing these things. If your golfing opponent jingles his change at the top of your backswing, he can probably reach the part of your brain that responds instinctively to sudden noises; since you're on autopilot, you're helpless to stop your now-doomed swing.

By contrast, great performers never allow themselves to reach the automatic, arrested-development stage in their chosen field. That is the effect of continual deliberate practice—avoiding automaticity. The essence of practice, which is constantly trying to do the things one cannot do comfortably, makes automatic behavior impossible. It's certainly true that a great performer is able to do many things in his or her field with far fewer mental demands than a novice performer; an excellent pilot lands a 747 without breaking a sweat. But ultimately the performance is always conscious and controlled, not automatic.

Avoiding automaticity through continual practice is another way of saying that great performers are always getting better. This is why the most devoted can stay at the top of their field for far longer than most people would think possible. We'll examine this phenomenon more closely in chapter 10.

How does it work?

While it seems intuitively right that extensive deliberate practice would make someone very good, we cannot fully understand what's happening, and cannot put it to best use, unless we know how it works. What specifically is going on inside a person as a result of these activities? What changes? How can we help it along? We turn to these important questions next.

Chapter Six

How Deliberate Practice Works

The specific ways it changes us,
and how that makes all the difference

At this point the evidence seems strong that the right kind of practice can turn someone of unremarkable endowments into a much better, even exceptional performer. But we're still left wondering how it happens. Until we understand that, the theoretical framework can't be entirely persuasive, and we cannot apply it in the most effective way. It would be like knowing that an engine is what makes a car go—extremely important to know, but if we don't understand how the engine works, we can never make the car go faster or run more efficiently. So—what makes deliberate practice work?

In general, we've seen that practice is all about pushing ourselves just beyond what we can currently do. Now we need to get more specific. We need to know which systems, physical or mental, the great perform ers overstrain and build up. It turns out the answer is the same whether we look at business or sports or any other field, and it isn't what you might expect.

Indeed, the most important effect of practice in great performers is that it takes them beyond—or, more precisely, around—the limitations that most of us think of as critical. Specifically, it enables them to perceive more, to know more, and to remember more than most people. Eventually the effects go beyond even that. Many years of intensive deliberate practice actually change the body and the brain. There's a good reason why we see the world's great performers as being funda-mentally different from us, as operating on a completely different plane. It's because they are and they do. But they didn't start out that way, and the transformation didn't happen by itself.

Let's examine each of the major ways deliberate practice changes a person.

Perceiving More

In his book *Blink,* Malcolm Gladwell describes the uncanny ability of Vic Braden to predict when a tennis player is going to double-fault. You get two chances to make a legal serve in tennis, and if a player had faulted on the first attempt, then on the second serve, at a moment after the player had tossed the ball into the air but before he or she had hit it, Braden would predict whether it would be a fault, and he was almost always right. Braden was then a very famous tennis teacher, having spent a long career as a professional player. In Gladwell's book, Braden says he's baffled by this ability, has no idea where it comes from. Gladwell does not venture to explain it and presents it as an intriguing mystery.

No research seems to have been conducted on Braden, so we can't say for sure how he did it. But as it happens, research on other excellent tennis players shows that in general they know where a serve is going to go earlier than average players—like Braden, they know even before the ball is hit—and explains quite clearly how they do it. This is impor-tant because it's a good example of how most of us misunderstand what makes exceptional performers so good.

A top-ranked male tennis player will serve the ball at speeds ap-proaching and occasionally exceeding 150 mph. (Andy Roddick seems to hold the record in competition, 155 mph.) At that speed, the ball will travel from the server's racket to the opponent's service line in just over a quarter of a second. Most of us, facing such a serve, would have a hard time turning our heads fast enough to watch it shoot past us. Yet top players routinely return those serves. The conclusion we tend to draw is that top players have incredible reaction times, enabling them to watch that ball come at them and get themselves in proper position in a quarter of a second.

Top professionals do indeed have very fast reaction times, and reaction speed can be improved with practice, so professionals work on it. The problem is that improvements in reaction speed follow what scientists call a power law (because there's an exponent in the formula) and what the rest of us call the 80-20 rule. That is, nearly all the improvement comes in the first little bit of training. After that, lots more practice yields only a little additional improvement. Top tennis pros have all pushed themselves to the point where it's tough to achieve any more reaction speed. The very best, however, have found a way to get around that limitation.

Researchers showed tennis players films of opponents serving at them, and used sophisticated equipment to track precisely their eye movements. Average players focused on the ball. But in the brief period between the start of the serving motion and the moment when the racket hits the ball—the period when Braden could detect the impending fault—the best players weren't looking at the ball. They were looking at the opponent's hips, shoulders, and arms, which foretold where they would hit the ball. The researchers then stopped the film at the moment of contact and asked the test subjects where the serve was going to go. The average players, being focused on the ball, had no idea. But the best players knew, and as a result, they could start positioning themselves to return the serve even before the serve was hit. By the time the ball landed, they were already there.

They had found a way to react faster without improving their reaction time.

Researchers have uncovered the same phenomenon in many kinds of sports and in a wide range of other activities. Top performers can figure out what's going to happen sooner than average performers by *seeing more* in badminton, cricket, field hockey, squash, and volleyball. Beyond sports, we see a similar result in the mundane but instructive field of typing. Why, specifically, can some people type so much faster than most? As in tennis, a person can go only so far in increasing reaction speed. The very fastest typists achieve their advantage by looking farther ahead in the text, which enables them to keep moving their fingers into place for the next keystroke just a little bit ahead of time (and, in particular, to hit successive letters typed with opposite hands especially fast, which is their most effective way of outrunning average typists). When researchers prevented top typists from looking farther ahead in the text, they performed scarcely better than novices.

Sometimes excellent performers see more by developing better and faster understanding of what they see. For example, accomplished and novice drivers were tested for their reactions to hazardous situations; they were shown films of various dangerous incidents from the driver's perspective. Again, the accomplished performers, facing the familiar limits on response time, didn't react any faster than the novices, but they understood what they were seeing much more quickly. The novices remained fixated on the hazardous situation much longer than the experienced drivers did, trying to comprehend it. The better drivers got it right away and thus had more time available to respond.

Even jugglers display similar abilities. Juggling—which is how most of us describe how we manage our lives—is a skill of continual monitoring, watching the balls and making constant tiny adjustments. Good jugglers don't need to see the whole path of the balls. When their vision is restricted, they can make the necessary adjustments as long as they can see just the apex of each ball's trajectory. Though seeing very little, they see more than average jugglers and understand all they need to.

Time and again we see the same themes, and so far we have considered just one type of situation in which top performers see more—cases requiring rapid responses. In fact the superior perception of experts shows up in many other ways.

Consider, for example, the reading of X-rays. Reaction time doesn't play an important role, but the stakes can be extremely high. In a study, expert radiologists and first- to fourth-year residents were asked to examine several X-rays, taking as long as they wanted, and to give their diagnoses and mark what they considered the problematic areas on the X-rays. The sample X-rays used in the study showed various serious problems, such as multiple tumors or a collapsed lung.

It shouldn't be surprising that the experts performed better; they were far more likely to spot the collapsed lung, for instance. But why? The middle lobe of the lung was collapsed and produced a dense shadow, but this feature could lead to a diagnosis of a tumor. The correct diagnosis required doctors to also see subtler cues, such as hyperinflation of the adjacent lobes. In marking the X-ray films, the experts picked out more specific features that were significant; they saw more clues to help them solve the puzzle of diagnosis. They also discriminated more finely. For example, the film showing tumors had a few hazy spots on it. The residents saw them as "general lung haziness" and figured they indicated fluid in the lungs, a sign of congestive heart failure. The experts saw correctly that each spot was a tumor.

The experts did not have sharper eyes in the usual sense. They were all looking at the same films and could see them just as clearly. The difference wasn't literally what they saw. It was what they perceived.

The superior perception of top performers extends beyond the sense of sight. They hear more when they listen and feel more when they touch. Highly trained pilots and apprentice pilots were asked to listen to a dialogue between pilots and air traffic controllers, and then to choose a diagram that best represented the situation they had just heard being talked about. The well-trained pilots were twice as good. Musicians are much better than nonmusicians at detecting very small differences in pitch and loudness of notes. Everyone in these studies is hearing the same things, but through years of practice, some are perceiving more.

The relevance of these findings for business seems obvious. Specifically, we can abstract from the research a few ways, directly applicable in business, that top performers perceive more.

They understand the significance of indicators that average performers don't even notice.

Just as top tennis players look at the server's body, not at the tennis ball, excellent performers in other fields have learned to spot nonobvious information that's important. Sometimes these signals are profound and become widely known. More than thirty years ago, when Wal-Mart had a very different reputation for employee relations than it does today, Sam Walton found an innovative way to gauge customer satisfaction. He realized that the best indicator of how happy his customers were was to measure how happy his employees were; the way managers treated the employees was the way employees would treat the customers (a lesson the company might want to reflect on).

More often these indicators are small but telling. Certain retail executives have been known to survey the oil stains in a store's parking lot to see how well the customers are maintaining their cars and thus gauge their financial condition. In the 1980s, when fitness was a heavily hyped trend, a business research firm dug through clothing sales statistics and found that the sales volume of clothing size extra-large and larger was increasing fast, an early tip-off that America was getting fatter, not fitter. Laura Rittenhouse, an unusual type of financial analyst, counts the number of times the word *I* occurs in annual letters to shareholders from corporate CEOs, contending that this and other evidence in the letters helps predict company performance (basic finding: Egomaniacs are bad news).

Often these nonobvious indicators are well-guarded secrets. Some hedge funds, for example, use mathematical models built on reliable relationships that the fund owners have discovered in the financial markets. Renaissance Technologies uses such models, and founder James Simons has for several years made more than $1 billion a year personally from the fund. If Renaissance's proprietary models were to become widely known and applied, the fund's advantage would disappear, so it's understandable that Simons doesn't like to talk about them. More generally in business and other fields, nonobvious indicators may be so valuable that most of us never know about them.

In general, regardless of whether indicators are secret, developing and using them requires extensive practice. For example, if you play tennis, you now know one of the ways that pros return serves so well. Yet you probably won't be able to do much with that information the next time you're on the court because you haven't spent hundreds of hours learning how to read the subtle movements of your opponent's hips, shoulders, and arms. Most of the indicators used by top performers require practice to be of any use.

They look further ahead.

When excellent musicians or typists look further ahead on the page than average performers do, they are literally looking into their own future. Knowing what lies ahead for them, they prepare for it and thus perform better. They may be looking only one second ahead, but for them that extra moment makes all the difference. In other fields the time periods are obviously much greater, and the advantages just as important.

This is not about fortune-telling, or hiring Nostradamus or an astrologer. Much of the power of looking further ahead comes from the simple act of raising one's gaze and getting a new perspective, and doing it not once or occasionally, but using practice principles to do it often and get better at it. When was the last time you, in your working role, participated in a deep discussion about the state of your business five years from now? How about fifteen years from now, including a

look at the future of your business's environment, competitors, regula-
tors, and other factors? Such discussions rarely happen below the level
of the CEO, yet the experience of excellent performers suggests they
offer advantages for everyone.

A few companies look far into the future as a matter of policy. Japan
scholar John Nathan recalls meeting with Panasonic founder Konosuke
Matsushita, widely regarded as one of the twentieth century's greatest
businesspeople; they were in a small boat on a pond at the company
compound. Matsushita clapped his hands once. Within moments, several large fish rose to the surface, recognizing the signal for feeding.
"These fish understand the long term," he said. "They live for a hundred
years." Matsushita looked further ahead than that: He had a five-
hundred-year plan for his company, which is now more than ninety
years old and remains powerful in the notoriously volatile electronics
industry.

Oil companies look further into the future than most because they
must. Negotiating the rights to an oil field may take many years, then
developing it may take another decade, and with luck it will produce
oil for decades more. That's why major oil companies routinely look at
forecasts of oil supply and demand one hundred years from now. The
best ones look beyond the numbers to see possible causes and effects.
For example, Shell's scenario planning process famously prepared it
for the Arab oil embargo of the 1970s. No scenario told Shell's managers the embargo would happen, since scenarios are thought exercises,
not predictions. But one of the scenarios the strategy group cooked up
envisioned an accident in Saudi Arabia that raised the price of oil, caus-
ing Arab producers to rethink why they set prices as they did. Shell
managers carried the analysis further and realized that Arab producers,
angry with the United States for its support of Israel in the Six-Day War,
might believe they could serve many purposes at once by launching an
embargo or restricting supply.

Because they had done the exercise, Shell managers could see how events might lead to an embargo, and when it happened, they were much better prepared than their competitors to respond. They had seen this movie already, so they slowed refinery expansion and adapted their refineries to handle many types of crude, while competitors vacillated. The common view in the industry is that Shell came through the oil shock far better than any other major producer.

These days it's common to question whether looking further ahead is worth the effort, since short-termism seems rampant. The conventional view is that no one is looking past the next quarter. But like much conventional wisdom, this just isn't so. Look at the stock tables any day and you'll find plenty of companies, many of them in biotechnology or infotech, with no profits and no prospect of profits anytime soon, yet with considerable share prices. Investors are valuing these companies by looking years into the future. Fashions in the market come and go, but the future always counts, and looking further into it—rationally—is always an advantage.

They know more from seeing less.

This ability is essential for success in every real-life domain because we never have as much information as we want. Getting information pushes at the two constraints everyone faces: It takes time and costs money. Making sound decisions fast and at low cost is a competitive advantage everywhere.

Top performers, through extensive practice, learn this ability for decisions that are most critical in their field. Police officers learn how to decide in a split second whether to shoot. Quarterbacks learn to decide from very few cues whether to throw the ball, and if so, where. Even in business, where linebackers aren't running at you, deciding fast with sparse information is often an advantage. That's easiest to see on Wall Street, where a difference of thirty seconds can turn a winning trade into a losing one, but it's also true in other businesses where the time demands aren't quite so intense. Jack Welch, who considered people decisions the heart of his job as CEO, would sometimes make them very quickly. He met a young GE auditor named John Rice at a lunch and recalls, "I liked him instantly." A presentation Rice gave impressed Welch, who gave Rice "a battlefield promotion" on the spot. From that career turning point, Rice became one of GE's biggest stars and a vice chairman of the company by age fifty. Welch didn't know much about Rice when he set him on the path, but he knew enough. And he knew it because intensive, disciplined people evaluations had been central to Welch's career for decades.

They make finer discriminations than average performers.

It was said of Charles Revson, the entrepreneur who built Revlon into a dominant cosmetics firm, that he could distinguish several different shades of black, a particularly difficult skill even among people who work with colors. That ability is a metaphor for making evaluations of every kind. For example, it's one thing to say that a manager is "good with people." It's another to ask whether a manager notices when a direct report seems no longer challenged by his or her job. If so, is that seen as a problem or an opportunity? What responses are proposed? Of these, how effective or ineffective do they seem, and which, if any, are applied? It's a matter of seeing black versus seeing five shades of black, and it works in evaluating people, situations, proposals, performances, products, or anything else. In each case, seeing differences that others don't see is another way of perceiving more.

Note that all these crucial abilities are clearly results of training and practice. We know this because in many cases they are abilities that those in a given field work on diligently, and that instructors try hard to teach. We know it also because research shows that these abilities generally don't transfer beyond the field in which they were learned. We may be tempted to say, for example, that an excellent musician "has a good ear," meaning an ability to make fine distinctions. But research shows that musicians who can distinguish extremely fine differences in music tones are no better than average in distinguishing different tones in speech. Deliberate practice works by helping us acquire the specific abilities we need to excel in a given field.

Knowing More

It may seem painfully obvious that great performers know more than average ones; we expect a great investor, for example, to know much more about his or her area of investing than average investors do. But it isn't nearly as obvious as it may seem, and in fact there was a time when many researchers believed it was not true. A bit of what they believed probably still resides in what most of us think.

These researchers thought that great performance came not from superior knowledge but from superior reasoning methods and reasoning power. You didn't really have to know much about a field if you knew the best ways to analyze a problem and think it through, and you needed to know even less if your analysis and reasoning power could be juiced by a computer. This line of thought was especially popular in the early days of computers, from the 1950s to the 1970s, when scientists were searching for ways to create intelligent machines and anything seemed possible. So heady was their ambition that in 1957 two scientists (Herbert Simon and Allen Newell) announced a computer program they called the General Problem Solver. It didn't know anything about anything in particular, but it possessed rules of logic and problem-solving strategy that could, in theory, be applied universally. It never did solve any real-world problems, but it showed the direction of much scientific thinking: You didn't need specific knowledge as long as you had a sufficiently powerful intellectual engine.

Eventually researchers began to realize that knowledge-free computing power wasn't producing the results they'd hoped for. To see how their approach wasn't working, consider one of the most celebrated attempts to produce artificial expertise, the quest for a successful chess-playing computer program. Here was the perfect setting for the knowledge-doesn't-matter approach. Just tell the computer the rules and the object of the game, and then turn it loose with its awesome speed and reasoning capacity, which no human could begin to match. The machine's triumph was inevitable.

The trouble was that humans kept winning. That was a big problem because chess researchers estimate that from any given position, even a top-ranked player needs about fifteen seconds to think through each possible move. By contrast, the early chess programs could try out thousands of moves per second. How could humans ever win? When Garry Kasparov, the world champion at the time, first played IBM's famous Deep Blue program in 1996, the computer was evaluating 100 million positions per second—and Kasparov still won. A year later the computer had been upgraded to evaluate 200 million positions per second, and Deep Blue finally won the six-game match: two games to one, with three draws.

Yet in light of its staggering advantages, why would the computer lose or draw even a single game against any player, ever? The answer is that the human possessed something the computer didn't, which was vast knowledge of chess—how previous masters had responded to particular positions in many different cases, and what kinds of choices generally produced what kinds of consequences. Eventually researchers from a broad array of fields realized where the secret lay. "The most important ingredient in any expert system is knowledge," wrote three eminent scientists who work on expert computer systems (Bruce G. Buchanan, Randall Davis, and Edward A. Feigenbaum). "Programs that are rich in general inference methods—some of which may even have some of the power of mathematical logic—but poor in domain-specific knowledge can behave expertly on almost no tasks." Their conclusion: "In the knowledge resides the power."

As it happened, other researchers were arriving at the same place by

a different route, though they also were studying chess. A Dutch psychologist named Adriaan de Groot compared world-class players with
good club-level players and found, surprisingly, that the world-class
players didn't consider more possible moves than the less-accomplished
players, nor did they search any deeper (more moves into the future),
nor were their rules of thumb for choosing moves any different. In sum,
their intellectual engines didn't seem to be turning any faster. So what
made them better?

Part of the answer, which seems to apply in every domain, is that
they had more knowledge about their field. In chess, researchers have
found (using a method I'll describe a little later) that master-level players possess more chess knowledge than good club-level players by a
huge margin, a factor of ten to one hundred. Just as important, top performers in a wide range of fields have better organized and consolidated
their knowledge, enabling them to approach problems in fundamentally different and more useful ways. For example, accomplished physicists and beginning physics students were given two dozen physics
problems and asked to sort them by type of problem. The beginners
sorted the problems according to their most obvious features, such as
whether they involved friction or an inclined plane. The more expert
physicists sorted them by the basic principles—say, Newton's second
law—that would be needed to solve them.

Other studies have replicated this finding in many other fields.
Expert psychological counselors sort statements from patients according to the factors most relevant for choosing therapy, while novice
counselors sort by superficial details. Commercial fishermen sort the
creatures they haul out of the ocean by criteria with high practical
relevance, such as behavior or commercial value; inexperienced fishermen sort the creatures by appearance. In general, the knowledge of top
performers is integrated and connected to higher-level principles.

The same phenomena seem apparent in business. Many companies work hard to give their top performers the widest possible knowl-

edge by assigning them to many jobs that are different in nature and location—operating jobs, staff jobs, all around the world—and in this way the top performers have typically learned several, and sometimes all, of the most important parts of the business.

It's particularly significant that many of the best-performing companies explicitly recognize the importance of deep knowledge in their specific field, as opposed to general managerial ability. The distinction is the same as the one that computer scientists were dealing with years ago as they tried to create the General Problem Solver; America's business community followed much the same journey. The top business schools and many of the leading companies tried for decades to turn out excellent general managers, people who could land at virtually any organization and whip it into shape through the sheer power of the techniques they had learned. They didn't need to know much about the specific business, went the theory; they just needed to know the strategies for solving business problems.

But it turned out that wasn't how management worked at many of the most successful companies. When Jeff Immelt became GE's chief in 2001, he launched a study of the best-performing companies worldwide—those that had grown much faster than the economy for many years and had produced excellent returns for shareholders. What did they have in common? One key trait the study found was that these companies valued "domain expertise" in managers—extensive knowledge of the company's field. Immelt has now specified "deep domain expertise" as a trait required for getting ahead at GE. He explained to the *Harvard Business Review:* "The most successful parts of GE are places where leaders have stayed in place a long time. Think of Brian Rowe's long tenure in aircraft engines. Four or five big decisions he made—relying on his deep knowledge of that business—won us maybe as many as 50 years of industry leadership. The same point applies to GE Capital. The places where we've churned people, like reinsurance, are where you will find we've failed."

Building and developing knowledge is one of the things that deliberate practice accomplishes. Constantly trying to extend one's abilities in a field requires amassing additional knowledge, and staying at it for years develops the critical connections that organize all that knowledge and make it useful. It must be noted, by the way, that the central importance of knowledge to great performance poses serious difficulties for the theory that great performance arises from innate talent, since no one is born with a vast fund of knowledge about anything.

The crucial role of knowledge demands that great performers develop one other key trait. After all, what good is a ton of knowledge if you can't remember it and bring it to bear at the critical moment?

Remembering More

You'll recall the description in chapter 3 of research on the memories of chess players. Expert players could look for just a few seconds at a chessboard with a real chess position, including as many as twenty-five pieces, and recall it perfectly, while novices could look at the same board and recall the places of only five or so pieces; but when the chess positions were random, experts could recall scarcely more than the novices. The conclusion was that top-ranked chess players did not possess incredible general memories but did possess an amazing ability to remember real chess positions. The question that we didn't address then but that begs for an answer is, how do they do it? How, specifically, are they able to remember so much? More generally, how can great performers in every realm recall more than would seem possible? Jack Nicklaus in his playing days could reportedly remember every shot he had hit in every tournament. Successful businesspeople often remember specific numbers from long-ago financial statements. Researchers find that excellent performers in most fields exhibit superior memory of information in their fields. What's the explanation?

Part of the answer came from the same research that produced

that remarkable finding about the chess players. The experiment—
presenting a chess position for a few seconds and then asking experts
and novices to recall it—looked like a straightforward test of short-term
memory. That's the type of memory in which we hold information very
briefly, and if we're distracted by some other demanding task, we forget
what we were trying to remember. Many decades of research have
shown that average short-term memory holds only about seven items.
The capacity of short-term memory doesn't seem to vary much from
person to person; virtually everyone's short-term memory falls in the
range of five to nine items.

As noted, the chess researchers found that the masters possessed
only average short-term memories when it came to recalling randomly
arranged pieces. Arguably more striking was their finding that even
with real chess positions, the masters had only average short-term
memories in that they recalled only five to nine "items," just like the
novices. The difference had to be in what those "items" were.

The researchers proposed what has become known as the chunk
theory. Everyone in the experiment remembered more or less the same
number of chunks of information. For the novices, a particular piece
on a particular square was a chunk. But for the masters, who had studied real positions for years, a chunk was much larger, consisting of a
whole group of pieces in a specific arrangement.

The difference is much like the difference between letters and words.
Imagine that you knew all the letters of the alphabet but had no idea
that they could be assembled into words. Then suppose you were shown
for five seconds an arrangement of letters—let's say "lexicographer"—
and were asked to remember the letters in the correct order. Since you
would see just a bunch of letters, you'd have a hard time remembering
more than the first seven or so. But in reality you recognize those letters as a word you're familiar with—and a thirteen-letter word at that—
so you can easily remember all those letters in the correct order. You
wouldn't need to study them for the full five seconds; a half-second

would be plenty. Though you'd have to think a bit, you could even repeat the whole string of letters backward.

When top-level chess players look at a board, they see words, not letters. Instead of seeing twenty-five pieces, they may see just five or six groups of pieces. That's why it's easy for them to remember where all the pieces are. The analogy can be carried further. You'll recall from our previous discussion of knowledge that the very best players know ten to a hundred times more than good club players. These chunks are the units of knowledge. Researchers estimate that good club players have a "vocabulary" of about 1,000 chunks, while the highest-ranked players have a vocabulary of 10,000 to 100,000.

The chunk theory is compelling and valuable, and it can be applied very widely. But as an explanation of the many remarkable memory feats of top chess players, and, by extension, of top performers in any field, it has some problems. It does fine in explaining the immediate recall of quickly presented chess positions, which are presumed to be stored in short-term memory; storing larger chunks enables expert players to overcome that type of memory's inherent limits. But short-term memory—obviously—doesn't last long and washes out if your mind turns to something else. That's why you have to write down a phone number as soon as you hear it, and if the doorbell rings in the meantime you've probably lost it.

But now think of those chess players who play ten simultaneous games blindfolded. They can't be holding all those chessboards in short-term memory because if they were, each time they turned to the next board they'd forget the one they were just thinking about. And they can't be using long-term memory because, at least as that type of memory is conventionally defined, storing and retrieving information fast enough and reliably enough to use in a chess game is not possible. So how do these expert players do it? The answer helps to explain the exceptional performance not only of top chess players but also of the best doctors making diagnoses, computer programmers writing software, architects designing buildings, executives choosing strategies, and any other excellent performer.

All these people have developed what we might call a memory skill, a special ability to get at long-term memory, with its vast capacity, in a fast, reliable way. They aren't using short-term memory or traditionally defined long-term memory. The researchers who first proposed this explanation, Anders Ericsson and Walter Kintsch, called it long-term working memory. Other researchers have called it expert working memory. To understand its critical element, remember the story of SF, the yelling runner who was able to recall extraordinarily long lists of random digits. He did it by relating the digits to numbers in forms that were meaningful to him; for example, he recalled the digits 4 1 3 1 in the form 4:13.1, a time for running the mile. He had created what's called a retrieval structure, a way of connecting the data to concepts he already possessed.

SF was trying only to recall digits. He had no larger objective, so he created a retrieval structure from concepts that just happened to be available to him and had nothing to do with his task. In the real world, the great power of long-term working memory—the reason it distinguishes the best performers—is that it's built on a retrieval structure connected to the very essence of the activity. Indeed, top performers' deep understanding of their field becomes the structure on which they can hang the huge quantities of information they learn about it.

To illustrate, consider first a simple research study involving two groups: devoted baseball fans and casual observers of the game. Both groups were given an engagingly written description of a half-inning of a game. Later, the devoted fans were much better able to recall the events that mattered to the game's outcome—advancing runners, preventing runs scored, and so on. The casual observers tended to remember colorful but irrelevant details, such as the crowd's mood and the weather. The fans' high-level knowledge of the game provided a framework on which to hang the information they had read.

That finding applies generally: Top performers understand their field at a higher level than average performers do, and thus have a superior structure for remembering information about it. The best medical diagnosticians remember more about individual patients because they use the data to make higher-level inferences for diagnoses than average performers do. The best computer programmers are much better than novices at remembering the overall structure of programs because they understand better what they're intended to do and how. Beginners at electronic engineering look at a circuit diagram and see components, while experts see major functional groups and remember them better. Rigorous research has shown all these and many more examples.

As for chess players, we now see that their amazing memory is based on more than just an ability to perceive pieces in groups. The best players also understand the strategic importance of each group, its role in attacking, defending, and distracting the opponent, and so on. In the letters-versus-words analogy, it isn't just that novices see letters while experts see words; the experts also know the meanings of the words.

It's clear that the superior memory of great performers doesn't just happen. Since it is built on deep understanding of the field, it can be achieved only through years of intensive study. It further requires consistently relating new information to higher-level concepts, which is hard work. It's also easy to see why experts' superior memory doesn't extend beyond their field of expertise: It is a central element of their expertise and can't be separated from it. Far from being a general ability, it is ultimately a skill that is acquired through many years of deliberate practice.

We've seen how extensive, well-structured, deliberate practice develops the specific abilities of great performers to perceive more, know more, and remember more, and how these abilities are critical to exceptional performance. But these aren't the only ways in which practice works. It exerts an additional, overarching influence that in a way is even more impressive: It can actually alter the physical nature of a person's brain and body.

This effect is not the obvious one in which a person's muscles get bigger as a result of weight training, for example, but rather involves characteristics that most people might think couldn't be changed. Endurance runners, for instance, have larger than average hearts, an attribute that most of us see as one of the natural advantages with which they were blessed. But no, research has shown that their hearts grow after years of intensive training; when they stop training, their hearts revert toward normal size. Athletes can change not just the size of their muscles but even the composition of them (the proportion of fast-twitch fibers to slow-twitch) through years of practice. Ballet dancers gain their ability to turn their feet out more than average people, and baseball pitchers their ability to extend their throwing arm farther back, through extensive practice at ages before their joints calcify.

Even brains can be changed. When kids start practicing a musical instrument, their brains develop differently—the cerebral cortex changes. Brain regions that hear tones and control fingers take over more territory, and the younger the age at which a person starts practicing, the greater the effect. The brain's ability to change is greatest in youth, but it doesn't end there. A study of London taxi drivers, who train rigorously for two years on average, found that their brains had grown in the areas that govern spatial navigation. Particularly important in such changes seems to be the buildup of a substance called myelin around nerve fibers and neurons, which work better with more myelin around them. The brains of professional pianists, for example, show increased myelination in relevant areas.

It's significant that myelination is a slow process. Building up myelin over a nerve fiber that controls, say, hitting a particular piano key in a particular way involves sending the appropriate signal through that fiber over and over. This process of building up myelin by sending signals through nerve fibers, which occurs in purely intellectual fields like business as well as in sports and music, needs to happen millions of times in the development of a great performer. In other words, the process of myelin development seems an exact parallel to how deliberate practice works, and illustrates in a new way why it takes many years of intensive work to become a top performer. Research on myelin is still in its early stages, but it appears possible that at the most fundamental, molecular level, myelin may be the connection between intense practice and great performance.

We've all had the powerful feeling, when watching or contemplating an extraordinary performer, that in some deep way this person is simply not like us. Whether studying Buffett's investing performance or listening to a recording of Pavarotti or watching Roger Federer hit a tennis ball, we cannot find a way to relate our own performance in their fields to what they do; we cannot imagine any conceivable path that would get us from here to there. That's why we always fall back on the same metaphors in describing such people: They're from another planet; they're superhuman; they're incredible.

What we've seen is that in a sense our natural reaction is right— great performers really are fundamentally different. Their bodies and brains are actually different from ours in a profound way. In addition, their abilities to perceive, organize, and remember information are far beyond anything that most of us possess. But we're wrong in thinking, as many do, that the exceptional nature of great performers is some kind of eternal mystery or preordained outcome. It is, rather, the result of a process, the general elements of which are clear.

There is in fact a path leading from the state of our own abilities to that of the greats. The path is extremely long and demanding, and only a few will follow it all the way to its end. No matter how far one goes, however, the journey is always beneficial and begins by applying the elements of the process. The question, then, is how.

Chapter Seven

Applying the Principles in Our Lives

The opportunities are many—
if we think about our work in a new way.

Benjamin Franklin was "America's first great man of letters" in the view of David Hume and many others, so we might naturally wonder how he came to be the extraordinary writer he was. His own account of it in his autobiography is well known—most of us read it in school—but in light of what we now know about how great performers develop, several elements of the story seem more significant and instructive than we may have realized.

As a teenager, Franklin seemed to think he wrote well enough, but then one day his father found an exchange of letters between Ben and a friend, John Collins, arguing a point back and forth. (The argument was whether women should be educated, Collins contending they were naturally unable to learn as much as men, Franklin taking the other side.) Ben's father first told his son what was good about his letters; they were better than Collins's in spelling and punctuation. Then he told him and showed him specifically how they were inferior: "in elegance of expression, in method and in perspicuity, of which he convinced me by several instances," as Franklin recalled. We must note in passing that when it comes to giving people evaluations—offering praise first, then supporting criticisms with examples—old Josiah Franklin could be a model for us all.

Ben responded to his father's observations in several ways. First, he found examples of prose clearly superior to anything he could produce, a bound volume of the *Spectator,* the great English periodical written by Joseph Addison and Richard Steele. Any of us might have done something similar. But Franklin then embarked on a remarkable program that few of us would ever have thought of.

It began with his reading a *Spectator* article and making brief notes on the meaning of each sentence; a few days later he would take up the notes and try to express the meaning of each sentence in his own words. When done, he compared his essay with the original, "discovered some of my faults, and corrected them."

One of the faults he noticed was his poor vocabulary. What could he do about that? He realized that writing poetry required an extensive "stock of words" because he might need to express any given meaning in many different ways depending on the demands of rhyme or meter. So he would rewrite *Spectator* essays in verse. Then, after he had forgotten them, he would take his versified essays and rewrite them in prose, again comparing his efforts with the original.

Franklin realized also that a key element of a good essay is its organization, so he developed a method to work on that. He would again make short notes on each sentence in an essay, but would write each note on a separate slip of paper. He would then mix up the notes and set them aside for weeks, until he had forgotten the essay. At that point he would try to put the notes in their correct order, attempt to write the essay, and then compare it with the original; again, he "discovered many faults and amended them."

What is so striking about Franklin's method is how closely it conforms to the principles of well-structured deliberate practice in the circumstances he faced. He did not have a teacher to guide him, but his father was able to identify some specific faults in his writing; Ben in effect created his own teacher by finding examples of prose that were beyond his own abilities. He could scarcely have chosen better; *Spectator* essays were exactly the type of engaging, topical, innovative writing that Franklin wanted to produce, and they were so good that the volume he studied is still widely available almost three hundred years later. So Franklin identified the aspects of his performance that needed to be improved and found a way to stretch himself, the essential core of deliberate practice.

Significantly, he did not try to become a better essay writer by sitting down and writing essays. Instead, like a top-ranked athlete or musician, he worked over and over on those specific aspects that needed improvement. First came sentence structure, which he attacked precisely in accord with deliberate practice principles. His method of summarizing and reformulating *Spectator* sentences one by one was designed ingeniously for that purpose. He repeated this routine at high volume, there being lots of sentences in an essay, and he got immediate feedback by comparing his sentences with the original. When he decided to work on another element of performance, vocabulary, he again designed a brilliant practice structure, versification, with high volume and immediate feedback. Note also that since he eventually converted his rhyming essays back into prose, he was continuing to work on sentence structure. His approach to a third element, organization, was again extremely clever in allowing him to stretch himself repeatedly on that specific skill while also maintaining the others.

One further feature of Franklin's approach to better writing is important to note. He pursued it diligently. When people today hear about what he did, they generally marvel not at the brilliance of his practice design but at his ability to carry it through. It seems like so much work. The truth is that in theory anyone could have followed his routine; anyone still can, and it would be highly effective. But nobody does it, not even students who are studying writing. And Franklin was not a student. He was then an apprentice in his brother's printing business, a demanding job that left him little free time. He practiced writing before work in the morning, after work at night, and on Sunday, "when I contrived to be in the printing-house alone." Raised as a Puritan, he knew he was supposed to be in church on Sunday, but "I could not, as it seemed to me, afford time" to go.

The details of how Franklin taught himself to write well are worth our attention for two reasons. First, they provide a particularly clear example of how deliberate practice works—in this case how it helped form one of the most effective and influential writers of English prose of his era. Second, they're an inspiring illustration of how to apply these principles on one's own in circumstances far from ideal—which unfortunately are just the circumstances in which most people in companies and many other organizations find themselves today.

We saw earlier how hostile to the principles of well-structured deliberate practice most companies seem. That's all the more puzzling when you consider how many high-profile organizations apart from businesses embrace these principles. We're awed by the performances of champion sports teams or great orchestras and theater companies, but when we get to the office, it occurs to practically no one that we might have something to learn by studying how some people became so accomplished. The U.S. military has made itself far more effective by studying and adopting these principles, and it funds some of the most important research in this field. But at most companies—as well as most educational institutions and many nonprofit organizations— the fundamentals of great performance are mainly unrecognized or ignored.

That's the reality at most organizations, though not all. We'll see in the next chapter how some organizations apply these ideas in diverse ways, and how they could do so even more. But since most organizations don't understand or apply these principles, and since most people aren't in a position to change how their employer operates, we'll look first at what individuals can do on their own, like Ben Franklin, to become much better in their fields.

Know Where You Want to Go

Step one, obvious yet deserving a moment's consideration, is knowing what you want to do. The key word is not *what,* but *knowing.* Because the demands of achieving exceptional performance are so great over so many years, no one has a prayer of meeting them without utter commitment. You've got to know what you want to do, not suspect it or be inclined toward it or be thinking about it. In the final chapter we'll look more closely into the mysterious question of where that commitment comes from. For now we'll assume that you're settled on what you want to achieve, even if it's only the next step in a general direction.

The first challenge in designing a system of deliberate practice is identifying the immediate next steps. In a few fields those steps are clear. If you want to play the piano, the exact skills you must learn and the order in which to learn them have been worked out by many generations of teachers. It's similar in highly structured professions; at least the initial steps in becoming an accountant, lawyer, or doctor are well established, and you have teachers to guide you.

But in the great majority of careers, and in the advanced stages of all of them, there is no published curriculum, no syllabus of materials that must be studied and mastered. In deciding which skills and abilities to work on, and how to do it, you're on your own. Most of us are completely unqualified to figure these things out by ourselves; we need help.

From this perspective we can see mentors in a new way—not just as wise people to whom we turn for guidance, but as experienced masters in our field who can advise us on the skills and abilities we need to acquire next, and can give us feedback on how we're doing. At least that's the ideal mentor, ideally used. Finding such a person isn't easy, but it's always possible to pursue the general principle: In all practice activities it's highly valuable to get others' views about what you should be working on and how you're doing.

The skills and abilities one can choose to develop are infinite, but the opportunities to practice them fall into two general categories: opportunities to practice directly, apart from the actual use of the skill or ability, the way a musician practices a piece before performing it; and opportunities to practice as part of the work itself.

Practicing Directly

In most jobs the notion of practicing directly is not well established, aside from maybe rehearsing a speech. But in fact the possibilities are surprisingly wide and deep. We can think of them in three general categories, based on models used in fields in which practice is accepted as critically important.

The music model.

In the classical tradition, a musician knows what he or she is going to play; the music is written down. What separates the greats from the rest is how well they perform that music. In business we find many analogous situations, far more than you might at first think. The most obvious involve presentations and speeches, and these form the one element of corporate life that is commonly practiced. But how well? These events can be extraordinarily important—a presentation to Wall Street analysts, to the board of directors, to your boss, to a congressional committee, or just to immediate colleagues can hold large consequences for you or your organization. Yet for most people, practice consists of perhaps a few run-throughs.

Think of all the ways it could be done much better. One could analyze the text of the talk and in each section determine the most important idea to be conveyed—passion, logical inevitability, common bonds with the audience, humor—and then work on each section repeatedly, constantly striving to express that key idea more effectively, with feedback after each repetition, either from a coach or by watching video. In the age of YouTube, it may be easy to find video of others giving similar types of presentations that one can then analyze and learn from, noting specifically how other speakers tried—well or badly—to convey the same key ideas that you want to put across.

Is this way more work than anyone you know has ever put into a presentation? Most likely. But it is exactly the type of preparation that great performers put into whatever they do.

Many other important elements of business life can be practiced similarly. One of the most dreaded tasks for many managers is giving job evaluations to their direct reports. This is a music-model task; you know what you want to convey, and the challenge is to convey it effectively. The message can be broken down into pieces and each piece analyzed for intent, then practiced repeatedly with immediate feedback from a coach or by video. Even being interviewed—by a prospective employer or by the news media—can be practiced in this way. After all, in those situations you probably know the key messages that you intend to convey, regardless of the questions you're asked.

We have bypassed the question of how these presentations or speeches get written. It's often said that anything you write is a performance, which suggests that writing may be considered a music-model activity. For straightforward written work, the multipart Ben Franklin technique would be appropriate; instead of emulating the *Spectator,* you would choose a superior letter to the shareholders, advertisement, blog entry, or other appropriate model. For spoken presentations, a particularly effective approach would be a juiced-up Ben Franklin technique: Watch a presentation that you consider especially well done and make notes of its various points; later, after you've forgotten most of it, use your notes to create a talk making the same points; deliver the talk and record it; then compare your video with the original.

The chess model.

Excellent chess players practice by studying positions from real games between top-level players, organized by various themes—openings, endgames, attacks, defenses, and many other categories that are far more refined. Thousands of books of such positions have been published. The practice routine is to study a particular position and choose the move you would make, then compare it with the move chosen by the master; if they're different, figure out why and which is better.

This is practice of a different type, but it still fulfills the requirements of well-structured deliberate practice: It is designed to meet the central demands of the field, in this case move selection, and can be further focused on the types of moves that need to be improved; and it involves high repetition and immediate feedback. Many elements of job performance can be improved through a similar approach.

In fact, the chess model has been used widely in business education for eighty years, but under a different name: the case method. Pioneered at the Harvard Business School, it is strongly analogous to chess practice: You're presented with a problem, and your job is to figure out a solution. Real life being the way it is, you often won't know whether the solution chosen by the case's protagonist was the best one possible, or whether yours was any better. But the process of focusing on the problem and evaluating proposed solutions is powerfully instructive, which helps explain why the case method is used by hundreds of universities around the world.

One of the great strengths of this approach is that it can be focused sharply on specific skills that need improvement, in keeping with deliberate practice principles. You might work in marketing for years and get only a couple of chances to market U.S. products in China, for example, so that's a skill you probably wouldn't be very good at. But in a short time you could study a dozen cases about marketing U.S. products in China. That's one step removed from actually marketing the products, but it puts you many steps ahead of anyone who has not studied that specific skill intensely and repeatedly.

One way to apply the chess model is to take business classes that use the case method. That option isn't always available, but it holds many advantages. Since the correct response to the case problem isn't always clear, it's helpful to hear the perspectives of other students and especially of the teacher, who may be the writer of the case. Classes also typically expose students to a lot of cases; students at the Harvard Business School study more than five hundred of them during the two-year program.

If you can't go to business school or take business classes, you can still apply the chess model ad hoc. For starters, many of the case studies used at famous business schools worldwide are for sale; you can buy them online and study them yourself. More generally, consciousness of the chess model changes the way you read the news or observe what happens in your own industry or the company where you work. The essence of the chess model is the question: What would you do? Each news event that you read about, each new development in your company or industry, is an opportunity for you to answer that question. Oil prices jump, consumer spending tanks, a rogue trader loses $7 billion, Apple introduces the iPhone—don't just read the news, imagine how it might affect the business you're in or want to be in, and answer the question: What would you do? Then comes a critically important step: Write your answer down and keep it. Remember, feedback is crucial to effective practice, and people have a tendency to misremember what they thought in the past; we almost always adjust our recollections flatteringly, in light of how events actually turned out. But there's no escaping a written record. Comparing your own what-would-I-do with the results of what the protagonist really did is the only way this exercise can yield genuine learning, and that learning can be considerable.

The sports model.

The practice of top athletes falls into two large categories. One is conditioning, building the strengths and capacities that are most useful in a given sport. NFL linemen build their leg muscles in a way that produces explosive power; tennis players work on stamina so they can still get to the ball three hours into a match. The other category of practice is working on specific critical skills—batting a baseball, throwing a football, hitting a golf ball out of the sand. A characteristic that many of these skills share is that they must be performed differently every time because the situations in which they're encountered are never the same. That's why this is different from the music model. For a pianist, the notes in Beethoven's *Moonlight Sonata* never change, but for a quarterback, no two passing situations are ever alike.

What are the analogs in business? For conditioning, we'll assume that your work makes no significant physical demands; if it does, the appropriate physical conditioning opportunities will be apparent. But if your work is information- and service-based, as most work in the developed world is, then conditioning means getting stronger with the underlying cognitive skills that you probably already have—basic math and accounting in financial jobs, basic science in engineering jobs, basic language skills in editorial jobs. In many cases this is stuff you learned in high school or college, and it's tempting to think you couldn't possibly benefit from revisiting it. But the truth is that these strengths, like physical strengths, decay if they aren't maintained.

Conditioning in this context can take various forms. It can mean getting out those old textbooks or handbooks and reviewing the fundamental skills that underlie your work, becoming faster, more facile, and more confident with them. For example, no matter how long you've worked in the world of investments, you will benefit from rereading Graham and Dodd's *Security Analysis,* a book you probably got when you started; and I guarantee you will learn something important that you'd forgotten. For people who write and edit, the same applies to Fowler's *Modern English Usage* and Strunk and White's *The Elements of Style*. Every field has classic guides that will always repay study, just as linebackers will always benefit from leg presses. The difference is that every linebacker from high school on up to the NFL does leg presses, while surprisingly few people in business practice the basic conditioning that supports all they do.

Conditioning can also be practiced with new material. Analyze the basic ratios in an unfamiliar financial statement with pen and paper, even though you have software that could do it all with one click. Do a value-based analysis of a stock. Pencil-edit a magazine article. You won't be learning new skills; you'll be building the strengths that make all your skills possible.

The second type of practice in the sports model, specific skill development, is based on focused simulation, and that concept can be applied widely in business, though doing it by oneself may be a challenge. Athletes spend much of their time working on particular skills that aren't like playing a piece of written music, which doesn't change, or like certain sports skills that are entirely under the athlete's control, such as pitching a baseball or serving a tennis ball. These other skills are difficult in part because they have one or both of two traits. First, they may require a fast response to an unpredictable action by the opponent—hitting a baseball or returning a tennis serve, for example. Second, they may be fluid and dynamic; a pass receiver may not be open when the quarterback throws the ball but may be by the time the ball arrives.

Unpredictable opponents, fast responses, dynamic situations—how very much like life in business. Practicing these situations can be difficult on your own because by their nature they involve other people. If you can get someone to help you practice a sales call or a negotiation, for example, by all means do so, being sure to remember the principles: trying to improve a specific aspect of your performance, high repetition, immediate feedback. But if you can't get anyone to help, you can do a great deal of this type of practice by yourself through the fast-growing world of business simulations. It's quite amazing what's available. Web-based or downloadable simulation games in marketing, stock trading, negotiating, corporate strategizing, and many other disciplines at several levels of sophistication are widely available, with more being created every day. They are a genuine advance in making this valuable type of practice easy and accessible.

Practicing in the Work

Opportunities to practice business skills directly are far more available than we usually realize, but even these aren't the only opportunities. We all face a different way to practice business skills, and that is by finding practice in the work itself. It is, to repeat, a different kind of activity. If you're holding a talk with your boss about your bonus target, you probably can't say, "Hold on—let's discuss that point five more times." But in that or any other situation you can do different things that will help make you much better. And they're all done in your head.

Researchers call these activities self-regulation. That term encompasses a broad range of behaviors, some of which are highly relevant here. Professor Barry J. Zimmerman, of City University of New York, and colleagues have studied these behaviors extensively, and he finds that the "properties of deliberate practice . . . have been studied as key components of self-regulation." Effective self-regulation is something you do before, during, and after the work activity itself.

Before the work.

Self-regulation begins with setting goals. These are not big, life-directing goals, but instead are more immediate goals for what you're going to be doing today. In the research, the poorest performers don't set goals at all; they just slog through their work. Mediocre performers set goals that are general and are often focused on simply achieving a good outcome—win the order; close out my positions at a profit; get the new project proposal done. The best performers set goals that are not about the outcome but about the process of reaching the outcome. For example, instead of just winning the order, their goal might be to focus especially hard on discerning the customer's unstated needs.

You can see how this is strongly analogous to the first step of deliberate practice. It isn't precisely the same; you are not designing a practice activity, but rather doing whatever the requirements of work may demand of you that day. But within that activity, the best performers are focused on how they can get better at some specific element of the work, just as a pianist may focus on improving a particular passage.

With a goal set, the next prework step is planning how to reach the goal. Again, the best performers make the most specific, technique-oriented plans. They're thinking of exactly, not vaguely, how to get to where they're going. So if their goal is discerning the customer's unstated needs, their plan for achieving it on that day may be to listen for certain key words the customer might use, or to ask specific questions to bring out the customer's crucial issues.

An important part of prework self-regulation centers on attitudes and beliefs. You may be thinking that figuring out specific goals and plans for what you'll be doing every day sounds hard. It is, and doing it consistently requires high motivation. Where does it come from? The best performers go into their work with a powerful belief in what researchers call their self-efficacy—their ability to perform. They also believe strongly that all their work will pay off for them.

During the work.

The most important self-regulatory skill that top performers use during their work is self-observation. For example, ordinary endurance runners in a race tend to think about anything other than what they're doing; it's painful, and they want to take their minds off it. Elite runners, by contrast, focus intensely on themselves; among other things, they count their breaths and simultaneously count their strides in order to maintain certain ratios.

Most of us don't do work with a significant physical element, but the same principle applies in purely mental work. The best performers observe themselves closely. They are in effect able to step outside themselves, monitor what is happening in their own minds, and ask how it's going. Researchers call this metacognition—knowledge about your own knowledge, thinking about your own thinking. Top performers do this much more systematically than others do; it's an established part of their routine.

Metacognition is important because situations change as they play out. Apart from its role in finding opportunities for practice, it plays a valuable part in helping top performers adapt to changing conditions. When a customer raises a completely unexpected problem in a deal negotiation, an excellent businessperson can pause mentally and observe his or her own mental processes as if from outside: Have I fully understood what's really behind this objection? Am I angry? Am I being hijacked by my emotions? Do I need a different strategy here? What should it be?

In addition, metacognition helps top performers find practice opportunities in evolving situations. Such people can observe their own thinking and ask: What abilities are being taxed in this situation? Can I try out another skill here? Could I be pushing myself a little further? How is it working? Through their ability to observe themselves, they can simultaneously do what they're doing and practice what they're doing.

After the work.

Practice activities are worthless without useful feedback about the results. Similarly, the practice opportunities that we find in work won't do any good if we don't evaluate them afterward. These must be self-evaluations; because the practice activities took place in our own minds, only we can know fully what we were attempting or judge how it turned out.

Excellent performers judge themselves differently from the way other people do. They're more specific, just as they are when they set goals and strategies. Average performers are content to tell themselves that they did great or poorly or okay. The best performers judge themselves against a standard that's relevant for what they're trying to achieve. Sometimes they compare their performance with their own personal best; sometimes they compare with the performance of competitors they're facing or expect to face; sometimes they compare with the best known performance by anyone in the field. Any of those can make sense; the key, as in all deliberate practice, is to choose a comparison that stretches you just beyond your current limits. Research confirms what common sense tells us, that too high a standard is discouraging and not very instructive, while too low a standard produces no advancement.

If you were pushing yourself appropriately and have evaluated yourself rigorously, then you will have identified errors that you made. A critical part of self-evaluation is deciding what caused the errors. Average performers believe their errors were caused by factors outside their control: My opponent got lucky; the task was too hard; I just don't have any natural ability for this. Top performers, by contrast, believe they are responsible for their errors. Note that this is not just a difference of personality or attitude. Recall that the best performers have set highly specific, technique-based goals and strategies for themselves; they have thought through exactly how they intend to achieve what they want. So when something doesn't work, they can relate the failure to specific elements of their performance that may have misfired. Research on champion golfers, for example, has uncovered precisely this pattern. They're much less likely than average golfers to blame their problems on the weather, the course, or chance factors. Instead they focus relentlessly on their own performance.

The final element of the postwork phase is affected by all the others and affects them in turn. You've been through some kind of work experience—a meeting with your team, a trading session, a quarterly budget review, a customer visit. You had thought about what you wanted to achieve and to improve, and it went however it went. Now: How do you respond? Odds are strong that the experience wasn't perfect, that parts of it were unpleasant. In those cases, excellent performers respond by adapting the way they act; average performers respond by avoiding those situations in the future. That stands to reason. Average performers go into a situation with no clear idea of how they intend to act or how their actions would contribute to reaching their goal. So when things don't turn out perfectly, they attribute the problems to vague forces outside their control. As a result, they are clueless about how to adapt and perform better next time. Little wonder that they'd rather just avoid going through anything like it again, which of course means they have zero chance of getting any better.

Since excellent performers go through a sharply different process from the beginning, they can make good guesses about how to adapt. That is, their ideas for how to perform better next time are likely to work. So it's hardly surprising that they are more likely than average performers to repeat the experience rather than avoid it. And when they do repeat it, we can now understand why they go into it with some of the prework traits and attitudes we observed: They approach the job with more specific goals and strategies, since their previous experience was essentially a test of specific goals and strategies; and they're more likely to believe in their own efficacy because their detailed analysis of their own performance is more effective than the vague, unfocused analysis of average performers. Thus their well-founded belief in their own effectiveness helps give them the crucial motivation to press on, powering a self-reinforcing cycle.

Deepening Your Knowledge

In addition to finding opportunities to practice skills directly as well as in the midst of their work, people in the business world can pursue one more category of activities that utilize the principles of great performance to get better at what they do. We've seen how deep domain knowledge is fundamental to top-level performance. You don't have to wait for that knowledge to come your way in the course of your work. You can pursue it.

It's crazy that in most jobs and at most organizations, there's little or no explicit education about the nature of the domain. Engineers, lawyers, accountants, and others go to school to learn the skills of their profession, but when it comes to the company, the industry, financial relationships, and how the business works, most people assume they'll just pick up what they need to know, and most organizations agree. In reality, maybe you'll pick up what you need to know or maybe you won't. But in light of the critical importance of domain knowledge, it's obvious that this offhand approach to acquiring that knowledge makes no sense.

Imagine the difference if you made domain knowledge a direct objective rather than a byproduct of work. If you set a goal of becoming an expert on your business, you would immediately start doing all kinds of things you don't do now. You would study the history of the business, identify today's leading experts, read everything you could find, interview people inside your organization and outside it who could provide new perspectives, track key statistics and trends. The exact steps would vary depending on your business, but it's quickly apparent that you could make yourself impressively more knowledgeable about your business than you are today, and probably do so in short order. With time, your knowledge advantage over others would become large.

The opportunity is richer than you may suspect. Michael Porter, the Harvard Business School professor who is one of the all-time great authorities on corporate strategy, prepares rigorously for his consulting assignments by studying the client company and its industry. He once said that with twenty hours of library research (this was pre-Internet) he could know as much about the business as the CEO did. Of course Porter has spent many years learning what data to look for, so maybe it would take you forty hours. That still looks like a high-return investment. Imagine what an advantage you would hold by gaining such knowledge, especially if your employer, like most, doesn't educate employees explicitly in the most important information about the company and industry.

As you add to your knowledge of your domain, keep in mind that your objective is not just to amass information. You are building a mental model—a picture of how your domain functions as a system. This is one of the defining traits of great performers: They all possess large, highly developed, intricate mental models of their domains.

The principle applies to all fields that are complex and demanding—corporate strategy, medicine, politics, and a great many others. For example, your mental model of the domain of driving, while adequate for your purposes, is probably quite sparse. You have a general understanding of how the car works, you're highly familiar with a few well-traveled routes, and you pay a bit of attention to gas prices. But a top-performing truck driver possesses an extremely rich mental model of the same domain. He understands in detail all the subsystems of his vehicle—mechanical, hydraulic, electrical—and how they interact. He knows hundreds of routes and their features, including speed limits, road conditions, service facilities, weight limits, weighing stations, police activity, gas prices, state licensing requirements, and many others. Most important, he understands the subtle ways in which all these shifting factors combine to influence his profitability.

For anyone, a rich mental model contributes to great performance in three major ways:

A mental model forms the framework on which you hang your growing knowledge of your domain.

We've seen how top performers can reach into their long-term memory in ways that ordinary performers can't, and how it isn't because they have exceptional memories but because they have exceptional knowledge of their domain. The organization of that voluminous knowledge in a mental model is what gives it so much power. A mental model not only enables remarkable recall, it also helps top performers learn and understand new information better than average performers, since they see it not as an isolated bit of data but as part of a large and comprehensible picture. For instance, an ordinary accountant might see a particular recent accounting rule change—Financial Accounting Statement 157—which requires companies to measure the riskiness of their assets in new ways, as a big, complicated pain in the neck that amends or deletes portions of forty-seven other statements. But a top accountant sees the change as part of a broad, post-Enron shift toward more detailed risk assessment, and understands who it helps, who it hurts, and why it was made.

A mental model helps you distinguish relevant information from irrelevant information.

That ability is valuable when you encounter new factors in a situation because it frees up mental resources to work on what's really important. In a study, top-performing pilots and apprentices listened to recordings of air-traffic control radio communications, and then were asked to recall what they heard. The apprentices actually recalled more of the "filler" words that had no practical significance than the top pilots did. But the expert pilots recalled far more of the important concept words. Because they heard the communications as part of a rich mental model, they could focus their brainpower on what counted.

*Most important, a mental model enables you to project
what will happen next.*

Since your mental model is an understanding of how your domain functions as a system, you know how changes in the system's inputs will affect the outputs—that is, how the events that just happened will create the events that are about to happen. Two groups of fire-fighters, novices and experts, were shown scenes of fires and asked what they saw. The novices saw what was obvious—the intensity and color of the flames. But the experts saw a story; they used their mental models to infer what must have led to the current state of the fire and to predict what was likeliest to happen next. Note that these inferences and predictions are more than just interesting. They are evidence that the experts are far better prepared than the novices to fight the fire.

A mental model is never finished. Great performers not only possess highly developed mental models, they are also always expanding and revising those models. It isn't possible to do the whole job through study alone. In many fields, much of this work must be done through deliberate practice activities or through metacognitive processes in the work itself, as we've discussed. But in addition, significant building and enriching of mental models can be done through study and other knowledge seeking, and it would be foolish to leave these tools unused.

You can do a great deal as an individual to apply the principles of great performance in your own life and work. Applying these principles is always beneficial. No matter how many steps on the road to great performance you choose to take, you will be better off than if you hadn't taken them. There is no hurdle to clear before the advantages start accruing. This is pure opportunity.

That's for you as an individual. Chances are you work in an organization. To really turbocharge the benefits of deliberate practice, the principles need to be applied organizationally as well as individually. It can be done, and the fact that it isn't done very widely makes the opportunity all the more valuable. That's our next topic.

Chapter Eight

Applying the Principles in Our Organizations

Few do it well, and most don't do it at all;
the sooner you start, the better.

Not all organizations want to be great. That's the hard truth. For those that do—that really do—the principles of great performance show quite clearly what it takes to get there. And for those enterprises that are paddling hard just to stay afloat, whose owners and managers may not feel they've got the luxury of thinking grandiose thoughts about greatness, these same principles can help make their performance much better. In fact, the principles of great performance can help improve such organizations to the point where they might actually dare to think about greatness. That is, the principles can do this if they're applied.

Yet the great majority of organizations don't apply these principles. In today's economy, that fact is more than just an opportunity. Applying the principles is becoming an imperative for all organizations that want to survive. We've seen in chapter 1 how the economy is increasingly based not on financial capital but on human capital, and how the abilities of the people in an organization—much more than traditionally important factors like economies of scale or patent protections—determine an enterprise's success or failure. And we've seen that, in a global economy, standards of performance are rising more quickly and more broadly than ever before, leaving subpar performers no place to hide. Those are reasons enough for organizations to start applying the principles of great performance in a big way. But there's more.

Today's best young employees, the ones on whom future success will depend, are demanding that employers help make them better performers. It seems that young people understood the new nature of today's economy before a lot of CEOs did, and they insist on employers who will keep developing them. Judy Pahren, senior vice president for development and diversity at Capital One Financial, which does a good job of applying the principles of great performance, says new employees consistently put continuous professional development at or near the top of their criteria for choosing an employer. Many other human resources chiefs report the same finding (and they all report that money is never among the top three criteria). General Electric, the best major company at applying the principles of great performance organizationally, is responding to the new environment by, among other things, getting high-potential employees to the company's famed Crotonville leadership development center much earlier in their careers than previously; CEO Jeff Immelt says that in attracting top prospects, "that's a strong selling point."

How the Best Organizations Apply the Principles of Great Performance

Organizations are finding that the advantages of building a big reputation for developing people are even greater than they may have thought. Such a reputation grants these companies "a first-pick advantage," as the RBL Group consulting firm calls it, an edge in attracting the cream of college and business-school students. By continually attracting the most promising graduates, and then developing them further, these companies become even higher-performing organizations, further enhancing their ability to attract the best—a virtuous cycle that makes a company more dominant every year.

The elite group of organizations that apply the principles of great performance follow several major rules.

Understand that each person in the organization is not just doing a job, but is also being stretched and grown.

That is, the best organizations assign people to jobs in much the same way that sports coaches or music teachers choose exercises for their students—to push them just beyond their current capabilities and build the skills that are most important. John Lechleiter, president of Eli Lilly, describes a typical model: about two-thirds of people development comes from carefully chosen job assignments, about one-third from mentoring and coaching (which we'll examine more closely), and a smidgen from classroom training.

Building people through job assignments seems obvious in theory, but in practice it's tough. Organizations tend to assign people based on what they're already good at, not what they need to work on. The merciless competitive pressure on every company makes it difficult to pull accomplished employees out of jobs they do extremely well and put them into positions where they may struggle. That's a tension every organization must deal with in order to become more successful.

No company assembles careers on the principles of great performance better than GE. It holds an advantage over most firms, since its breadth of businesses lets it offer a wider range of experiences than almost any other company. It uses that advantage for all it's worth to create some of the world's best-rounded and most sought after executives.

One of GE's secret developmental weapons, an example of the useful assignments it can hand out, is the job of running GE Transportation, the business that makes locomotives in Erie, Pennsylvania. Consider all the ways in which it can stretch a manager: Buying locomotives is a big decision for the business's customers, so the person running the shop—recently John Dineen, a twenty-one-year GE employee—gets experience dealing directly with CEOs of customer companies. The business is unionized, so he learns about labor negotiations. The product is complex, as is the supply chain—more learning that's broadly applicable. Erie is sufficiently remote and unglamorous that the business leader can develop without national media scrutiny. And if, heaven forbid, the leader is a washout, GE is big enough to handle the trouble without much trauma to the bottom line.

Dineen's prelocomotive career is a typical example of what GE can do and many other organizations strive for. He was a manager in the company's appliance and plastics businesses, both highly valued developmental posts, one of which makes consumer products and the other industrial products; he has worked in a couple of finance assignments, which also develop skills that are very important at GE; and he has held two large jobs in Asia, one staff and one line. You can't do much better than that.

Deliberately putting managers into stretch jobs that will require them to learn and grow is the central development technique of the most successful organizations. It won't work by itself; it requires the other practices described here to be effective. But these companies understand that for employees trying to improve, making real decisions in real time is the central practice activity that produces growth. Some firms follow detailed rules about which experiences are required; an executive may need to work in at least two territories, for example, or two lines of business. Others are more informal but still observe the principle.

Executives consistently report that their hardest experiences, the stretches that most challenged them, were the most helpful. A. G. Lafley, CEO of Procter & Gamble, was in charge of the company's Asian operations during a major Japanese earthquake and the Asian economic collapse. He says that's when he discovered that "you learn ten times more in a crisis than during normal times."

His crisis experiences happened by chance, but while crises can't be engineered, crisis experiences can be. A crisis was in progress at GE in 1988, when compressors in millions of GE refrigerators were found to be faulty and had to be replaced. CEO Jack Welch and human resources chief Bill Conaty decided to put Jeff Immelt in charge of the recall, though he had zero experience with appliances or with recalls. "It was a hurricane," Immelt says. "But Welch and Conaty knew exactly what they were doing. And there's no question I wouldn't be CEO today if I hadn't had that job."

Find ways to develop leaders within their jobs.

We've seen the value of domain expertise in any field. In business, that value seems to be increasing. Many top-performing organizations report new tension between their need to develop people by moving them through different jobs and the need to develop their expertise in certain domains by leaving them in jobs. This may result from the heightened competitiveness of a global economy; a division has a tough time competing when the boss moves on every eighteen to twenty-four months, a typical pattern in many companies. So the challenge is to give people the growth benefits of new stretch assignments without moving them into new jobs so often.

Eli Lilly is one of many companies trying harder to do that. One technique: short-term work assignments. Managers don't leave their jobs, but they take on an additional assignment outside their field of expertise or interest. That increases the burden on the employee, who is doing not just different work but additional work. Managers seem not to mind because they realize they've been identified for extra development. The company says the approach has been a big hit. Nokia is trying the same thing and reports a similar response.

Encourage their leaders to be active in their communities.

The advantages to the company are many. Most companies have enunciated values that include respect for the individual, good citizenship, and integrity. When company leaders also become leaders of charities, schools, and other nonprofits, they show their commitment to those values, encouraging and inspiring employees.

Other benefits are more pragmatic. Community leadership roles are opportunities for employees to practice skills that will be valuable at work. For example, most employees will never serve on the company's board of directors or on any major corporate board. But many of them can serve on a local nonprofit's board, and the experience is an excellent opportunity to develop strategic thinking, financial analysis, and many other skills. At General Mills, an explicit part of many employees' development plans as set by their bosses is to serve on a nonprofit board.

Understand the critical roles of teachers and of feedback.

We've seen that great performance is built through activities that are designed specifically to improve particular skills, and that in many realms teachers and coaches are especially helpful in designing those activities. At most organizations, nobody is in the role of teacher or coach. Employees aren't told which skills will be most helpful to them and certainly aren't told how best to develop them. But most top-performing organizations have explicit coaching and mentoring programs. At these enterprises, careful job assignments and other large-scale programs determine the general direction of an employee's development; mentors provide detailed advice on which subskills need attention right now. Many of the CEOs of these companies, when asked how they reached the top, tell similar stories about the importance of a few key mentors who consistently guided and helped them. Jeff Fettig, CEO of Whirlpool, is typical: "I am here today in part due to a handful of people who, before it was in vogue, provided coaching and mentoring to me early in my career. That helped me to develop."

The other side of this coin is feedback. We've examined at length the importance of frequent, rapid, accurate feedback for improving performance. Most organizations are terrible at providing honest feedback. The annual evaluation exercise is often short, artificial, and mealy-mouthed. Employees have no idea how well they performed and thus no prospect of getting better.

Yet nothing stands in the way of frequent, candid feedback except habit and corporate culture. Of course cultures can be formidable, but they can be changed. Any enterprise that wants a culture of true candor can have it, and there's no excuse for not having it. The best-performing organizations have exactly this kind of culture. For example, Immelt of GE says that the people who report to him "get coaching from me every time I see them."

Many of these companies could do even more to establish a culture of candor. A powerful tool with great potential for most organizations is the U.S. Army's after-action review. Colonel Thomas Kolditz, who runs the leadership development program at the U.S. Military Academy at West Point, says that for the past twenty-five years "it has literally transformed the Army." The concept is simple. After any significant action, in training or in combat, soldiers and officers meet to discuss what happened. They take off their helmets—a symbolic action indicating that "there's no rank in the room," as Kolditz says. "Comments are blunt. If the boss made a bad decision, often it's a subordinate who points that out." The session isn't about blaming; instead, it's "a professional discussion," as an army training circular puts it. Part of its strength is that it yields very complete feedback. "The genius of it is that the junior people always know what's going on," says Kolditz. "If you put them in a position to speak openly, they will."

The army has found another benefit of the after-action review: that when people really understand what happened, they're eager to try to do it better. This reinforces the principles of great performance. As the army training circular says, when an after-action review is done right, "not only will everyone understand what did and did not occur and why, but most importantly will have a strong desire to seek the opportunity to practice the task again."

The after-action review "is a very powerful process," Kolditz says. Its potential value to companies and other organizations is obvious. A number of firms have tried using it, usually with mixed results, and the problems are cultural. But cultures can be changed over time, and the best organizations will do the work necessary to change them in order to get the benefits of truly deep and broad feedback.

Identify promising performers early.

We've seen hints already, and will see in detail later, that an early start at development creates huge advantages. John Rice, the GE vice chairman whose career took off after Welch gave him a battlefield promotion, says, "Leadership capability can be evaluated on day one of employment." That's because day one isn't really day one for many employees, who have interned at GE for at least one previous summer, enabling the company to observe their performance. A telling indicator is how interns get others to work with them when they have absolutely no authority. Another signal that GE looks at, separate from internships, is whether someone played a team sport in college and what his or her role was.

Working on people's development early is a big change at most companies, where development programs were long reserved for an elite group several years into their careers. Many of the best-performing companies are trying to move past that. They believe that developing future leaders earlier than other companies creates a competitive advantage that lasts for decades, as their pipelines of high achievers become bigger, better, and more reliable.

Understand that people development works best through inspiration, not authority.

Deliberate practice activities are so demanding that no one can sustain them for long without strong motivation. How can an enterprise contribute to that motivation? The traditional answer was that it made people do what it wanted by firing, demoting, or otherwise punishing those who didn't. That never worked very well, and it works even worse in today's information-based economy, where most employees aren't turning wrenches but instead are using knowledge and relationships with results that may not be easily observed day-to-day. Try making them do what you say, or even telling them exactly what to do. A. G. Lafley of Procter & Gamble says, "The command and control model of leadership just won't work 99 percent of the time."

That is why a favorite word at many of today's best-performing companies is *inspire.* P&G runs a development program called Inspirational Leadership, which focuses explicitly on teaching leaders how to inspire colleagues. At American Express, everyone at or above the vice-president level attends a program called Leadership Inspiring Employee Engagement. These companies realize that they motivate best through a sense of mission. For some top performers, such as Medtronic or Eli Lilly, the mission is rooted deep in their history of saving lives or treating illnesses. For others, identifying or even creating a sense of mission requires a journey deep into the corporate soul. That trip is not for the faint-hearted. But it is mandatory for any organization that wants to motivate employees sufficiently to become world-class performers.

Invest significant time, money, and energy in developing people.

You don't develop people on the cheap, and you don't just bolt a development program onto existing HR procedures. The CEOs of top-performing companies agree that people development is at the center of their jobs. Indeed, the biggest investment involved may be the time of the CEO and other executives. At McDonald's, for example, CEO Jim Skinner personally reviews the development of the company's top two hundred managers. At GE, Immelt reviews the top six hundred. Bill Hawkins, CEO of Medtronic, says he spends 50 percent of his time on people issues, and many other top CEOs report similar percentages—making this the largest time commitment they have. Lots of companies claim they're interested in developing leaders, but the University of Michigan's Noel Tichy, a top authority on the subject, says testing their commitment is easy: "Just show me the CEO's calendar."

The CEO's time is only the beginning. Many of these chiefs note the "cascading" effect of what they do: As their direct reports see what the boss is focusing on, they also become devoted to developing people, as do their subordinates, and so on. Not that these companies rely solely on the power of example. Virtually all of them evaluate executives partly on how well they're developing people, including themselves. In American Express's highly rigorous system, for example, 25 percent of an executive's variable pay depends on people development.

Further expenses can be big, but no CEO seems to doubt their value. GE's Crotonville, a beautiful fifty-two-acre campus just north of New York City, obviously costs a bundle, and running thousands of managers through it every year costs even more. But "we fund it through good times and bad," says Immelt. "I learned that from Jack [Welch], and I still do it." Whirlpool decided a few years ago to upgrade its off-the-shelf development curriculum by developing its own. The program is now bigger than ever, and worth every cent. CEO Jeff Fettig says, "This is the single best investment we make in our company."

Make leadership development part of the culture.

Though executives at the best companies talk about their leadership development programs, they generally realize the term isn't quite right. Developing leaders isn't a program, it's a way of living. For example, honest feedback has to be culturally okay; at many companies it isn't. Devoting significant time to mentoring has to be accepted. Working for nonprofits has to be encouraged, not just tolerated. Such cultural norms can't be dictated on short notice; they have to grow over time. That's a major reason why GE is so widely regarded as the best at people development. Charles Coffin (CEO from 1892 to 1912) realized that GE's real products weren't lightbulbs or electric motors but business leaders; developing them has been the company's focus ever since.

Applying the Principles to Teams

Any organization that does all these things will build tremendous competitive advantages in its industry because its people will be developed to such an unusually high level. Every enterprise wants to be filled with A players, and rightly so. But that isn't enough.

After all, most people in an organization don't work alone. They work in teams, strictly or loosely defined. And a team's performance is emphatically not determined solely by the abilities of its members individually. Maybe you remember something called the World Baseball Classic, a tournament played by a group of national teams in the spring of 2006. You might suppose that no one could beat America at America's game, especially since the U.S. team was filled with undeniably great players—Roger Clemens, Derek Jeter, Alex Rodriguez, and Johnny Damon, among others. Yet the team didn't win the tournament and lost games to Mexico, South Korea, and—wait for it—Canada. Similarly, the 2004 U.S. Olympic basketball team, consisting entirely of NBA millionaires, finished third and lost to Lithuania, among other previously unknown hoops powers.

Turning groups of great individuals into great teams is a discipline in itself, which also operates on the principles of great performance. That's why the best organizations follow one additional rule:

Develop teams, not just individuals.

For example, Jeff Immelt recalls, "at the GE I grew up in, most of my training was individually based." But that led to problems. He'd attend a three-week program at Crotonville, but back at work "I could use only 60 percent of what I'd learned because I needed others—my boss, my IT guy—to help with the rest." And maybe they weren't on board. Now GE takes whole teams and puts them through Crotonville together, making real decisions about their business. Result: "There's no excuse for not doing it."

Applying the principles of great performance to team development is not conceptually difficult. The same basic elements that work for individuals—well-designed practice activities, coaching, repetition, feedback, self-regulation, building knowledge, and mental models—all work for teams as well. The problems are practical. They center on forces within the team that prevent it from realizing the benefits of the great-performance approach. Organizations that are the most successful at building team performance are especially skilled at avoiding or addressing potential problems that are particularly toxic to the elements of deliberate practice, such as the following:

Picking the wrong team members. Every team wants great individual performers, but combining them is a skill all its own, in business or any other domain. "Some of the worst teams I've ever seen have been those where everybody was a potential CEO," says David Nadler, a senior partner at the Oliver Wyman consulting firm, who has worked with executive teams at top global companies for more than thirty years. "If there's a zero-sum game called succession going on, it's very difficult to have an effective team."

Chemistry and culture are key. Henry Ford II successfully brought in the Whiz Kids, a preassembled team of U.S. Army managerial stars that included Tex Thornton, later founder of Litton Industries, and Robert McNamara, later president of Ford and then U.S. secretary of defense, when he sensed that Ford needed a revolution after World War II. The Whiz Kids had a record of working together effectively from their army days. But fifty years later, when Ford CEO Jacques Nasser correctly decided that the company needed another revolution, he stuck with the old-guard team already in place. Like most old guards, they weren't ready for a real revolution, and when push came to shove, Nasser got ejected. More seriously for Ford, the revolution didn't happen.

For a notably successful method of choosing team members, look at Worthington Industries, the Ohio-based steel processor. When an employee is hired to join a plant-floor team, he works for a ninety-day probationary period, after which the team determines his fate by vote. It works because much of the team's pay is at risk, based on performance, so team members are clear-eyed and unsparing in evaluating a new candidate's contribution. CEO John McConnell could be talking about teams at any level when he says, "Give us people who are dedicated to making the team work, as opposed to a bunch of talented people with big egos, and we'll win every time."

The most inspiring U.S. Olympic team ever, the 1980 hockey team that beat the Soviets at Lake Placid, was built explicitly on similar principles. Professional players weren't eligible back then. More fundamentally, coach Herb Brooks wanted to build a team on personal chemistry combined with extremely intensive practice. In the movie version of the story, called *Miracle,* Brooks's assistant looks at the coach's roster and objects that he has left out many of the country's greatest college players. To which Brooks responds with the essential mix-is-critical philosophy: "I'm not lookin' for the best players, Craig. I'm lookin' for the right players."

Low trust. Read the extensive literature on team effectiveness, or talk to people on teams in sports, business, or elsewhere, and it always comes down to this: Trust is the most fundamental element of a winning team. If people think their teammates are lying, withholding information, or plotting to knife them, nothing valuable will get done. Similarly, team members may not trust one another's competence. Such teams don't create synergy. They create its opposite, dysergy—two plus two equals three, with luck.

So-called dream teams may be in trouble right from the start because team members often have particular reasons to be distrustful. In sports settings, all-star teams are brought together only briefly from teams that spend the rest of the year trying to beat one another. Even if team members can set aside that antagonistic mind-set, they rarely have time to develop confidence in one another's behavior and abilities. It's similar in business: Even if team members aren't battling for the next promotion, someone is always getting moved or stolen away. "A major problem is that people are transient," says consultant Ram Charan. Especially on an all-star team, "there's all the headhunting, and there's a constant tug to have people pulled out of the team. Instability is a major issue." That's a big problem because trust by its nature is built slowly.

Many companies try to speed up the trust-building process. In the eighties there was a virtual epidemic of people falling backward off tables into the arms of coworkers as a way of learning trust. Maybe it even helped. Today consultants have developed many additional exercises that involve people sharing personal stories or revealing their personality type, based on the valid insight that reciprocal vulnerability is the beginning of trust. But the process can be rushed only so much.

In fact, trust is so fragile and so laboriously created that it may never extend very far in a top-level team. "Building a really high-performing executive team at the highest level is a mirage," says a famous management consultant who doesn't want his name used because this particular message is such a downer. "When such teams do exist, they'll consist mostly of two people, maybe three." It's just too hard to build trust more extensively at the top level, where everyone is supposedly a star.

And sure enough, the legendary top executive teams are almost always pairs. Think of Roberto Goizueta and Donald Keough at Coca-Cola in the eighties and nineties, or Tom Murphy and Dan Burke at Capital Cities/ABC from the sixties to the nineties, or Reuben Mark and Bill Shanahan at Colgate-Palmolive for two decades until 2005, or Warren Buffett and Charlie Munger at Berkshire Hathaway from the sixties to today. No one would have called those pairs dream teams back when they got together; at the time, most people had never heard of them. They all developed deep trust over many years and produced outstanding results.

Maybe you noticed something else about those teams: Each consists of a boss who became famous and a much less famous number 2 who devoted his career to the success of the enterprise. Such devotion is rare and points to another pathology that frequently sinks teams. . . .

Competing agendas. You don't often find examples of the best and worst executive teams involving the same person, but consider the case of Michael Eisner. For the first ten years of his reign at Disney, he and COO Frank Wells formed one of the great teams, saving a storied company and making shareholders rich. They were a classic top pair, with a clear number 1 and number 2, neither one famous outside the industry when they took the jobs. This productive partnership ended suddenly and terribly when Wells died in a 1994 helicopter crash.

Eisner then formed one of the most famously disastrous teams in recent history, bringing in überagent Michael Ovitz as president. He lasted only fourteen months. In the extensive postmortems, the overriding theme is conflicting business and personal agendas. Ovitz wanted to buy a major stake in Yahoo!, expand Disney's book and record businesses, and buy an NFL franchise, among other big ideas that Eisner dismissed as off-strategy. Ovitz also seemingly had notions of his own future—he spent $2 million remodeling his office—that did not sit well with Eisner. Bottom line: team failure.

It's a common problem. Just as great individual performers possess highly developed mental models of their domains, the best teams are composed of members who share a mental model—of the domain, and of how the team will be effective. Eisner and Ovitz held strongly conflicting models of Disney's domain and of their own team. More broadly, as noted, when everyone wants to be a CEO and has good reason to think it's possible, the conflicts can become overwhelming. And while it's easy to condemn the political hardball and hotdogging that result, don't be too quick to do so. After all, suppose you're toiling away beneath the world's radar and your boss gets fired—what happens to your career? Some companies even like to spotlight rising stars because it's good for the business; as these managers advance, employees want to follow them.

The challenge is to keep the inevitable personal agendas from becoming destructive. That's part of the leader's job. For example, Ameritech in the nineties had an all-star team of top executives that included Richard Notebaert, future CEO of Ameritech, Tellabs, and Qwest; and Richard Brown, future CEO of Cable & Wireless and EDS. Michigan business school professor Noel Tichy, who was advising the company on leadership development at the time, recalls that CEO Bill Weiss told the team bluntly every week that if he caught anybody trying to undermine the others, the guilty party would be fired.

Jack Welch used a different approach to managing potential successor conflicts at GE. He recalled his own miserable experience as one of the CEO finalists twenty years earlier, when the company promoted him and the other main contenders to jobs at headquarters, which politics soon turned into a steaming swamp. Two decades later, Welch kept his own top candidates in operating jobs hundreds of miles apart.

Even when ego-driven stars aren't fighting for the same job, a team can still be torn apart by another curse.

Unresolved conflicts. Colonel Stas Preczewski, coach of the army crew team at West Point a few years ago, faced a baffling problem. Through extensive testing he had determined the strengths and abilities of every rower on his team. He had measured each man's power on ergometers and had composed crews in every possible combination in order to calculate each member's contribution. He was able to rank his rowers objectively and precisely from best to worst. He then put the eight best in his varsity boat and the eight others, the weakest, in the junior varsity boat. The problem: The JV boat beat the varsity boat two-thirds of the time.

The situation is explained in a famous Harvard Business School case, which also notes that the varsity boat was full of resentment over who was contributing most, while the JV rowers, feeling they had nothing to lose, supported one another happily. But the case doesn't tell how Coach Preczewski solved his problem.

One day he lined up the varsity crew in four pairs. He told them they were to wrestle for ninety seconds. Only rule: no punching. "It was like the WWF," he recalls. When he stopped them, he noticed that no one was winning. Each man was discovering that his opponent was just as strong and determined as he was. Preczewski then had them change opponents and wrestle again. By the third round they were choosing their own opponents—"One guy would point at another and say, 'You!'" Preczewski says. On the fourth or fifth round, one of the rowers started laughing, and they all piled into a general brawl. Eventually someone said, "Coach, can we go row now?" From then on the varsity boat flew, and made it to the semifinals in the national tournament.

You probably can't order members of an executive team to wrestle, tempting though it may be. But there are other ways to discharge tensions that are crippling a group. These conflicts are the flip side of competing agendas; instead of being focused on the future, they typically linger from the past. Bringing them out into the open and then resolving them is one of the team leader's most important jobs. Doing it is an important element of dealing with a more general threat to team performance. . . .

Unwillingness to face the real issues. The usual metaphor is the elephant in the room. Former Eli Lilly CEO Randall Tobias called it the moose on the table. George Kohlrieser, a professor at the International Institute for Management Development in Switzerland, has developed the metaphor particularly well: "Put the fish on the table," he says. It's smelly, and cleaning it is messy work, but you get a good meal in the end.

Most people don't want to be the one who puts the fish on the table, especially on a team where it might not be culturally okay. "There's a veneer of politeness," says David Nadler, "or unspoken reciprocity—we won't raise our differences in front of the boss." Consultant Ram Charan describes a $12 billion division of ABB that was headed for bankruptcy. "One reason," he says, "was its culture of polite restraint. People didn't express their honest feelings" about the most important issues. The unit's leader turned it around by insisting that team members say what was really on their minds—though the first time, he had to endure sixty seconds of tense, angry silence after calling on an executive to explain why he was so clearly upset.

Jack Welch was one of the great champions of putting the fish on the table—confronting reality, as he says. Often overlooked were his efforts to make doing so easier for the top team. GE's dream team was and is the Corporate Executive Council, which used to meet at headquarters in a formal atmosphere with rehearsed presentations and little real discussion. Welch moved the meetings off-site, forbade prepared presentations, jackets, and ties, and lengthened the coffee breaks to encourage informal discussion, among other changes. At GE they call this social architecture. Business scholars believe it was a critical element in the success of Welch's revolution.

Applying the principles of great performance in an organization is no easier than doing anything else in an organization. It's hard. But in an increasingly competitive global economy, enterprises that want to survive and thrive will face little choice. If we suppose that every organization will sooner or later be trying to apply these principles, then it's important to remember that starting early confers a significant advantage. The effects of deliberate practice activities are cumulative. The more of a head start your organization gets in developing people individually and as teams, the more difficult it will be for competitors ever to catch you.

Chapter Nine

Performing Great at Innovation

How the principles we've learned
take us past the myths of creativity

It isn't true that everything can be commoditized. It just seems like it is.

One of the miracles of our networked world is that buyers know so much more about what they're buying, which is a major problem for the surprisingly numerous sellers who used to depend on customer ignorance. Most people still don't buy cars online, but most car buyers do shop online before buying; you see them walking into a dealership with a dealer's invoice, which they found online and printed out. That changes the balance of power. Prescription drugs have cost less in Canada for eons, but it didn't matter to the pharmaceutical industry before the Internet; now it does. Families with kids in college had long been floored by the exorbitant cost of textbooks in the college bookstore, but what choice did they have? Now they know they can often order the very same books from the United Kingdom for much less.

In the digital age, any products that can be compared will be compared, and any directly comparable products will be commoditized. Most brutally, this phenomenon takes the form of the reverse auction. An automaker, for example, needs a million injection-molded plastic parts. It designates eight suppliers as worthy to compete for the business, and tells them the specs, where and when the products will be needed, and the terms on which the winning supplier will be paid. Then it tells them all to get online Tuesday at eight AM and gives them an hour to beat the living daylights out of one another on price. When the bell rings at the end of the hour, the low bidder gets the business.

It's tempting to think that only a few low-value products could be bought this way, but in fact purchasers are finding ways to use this procedure for buying—that is, for commoditizing—all kinds of things, including high-value services. Tyco International (postscandal) used a reverse auction to hire a law firm to handle its product liability cases. A Kansas City–based firm called Shook, Hardy & Bacon won the business with an eighteen-month fixed-fee bid.

If you're wondering why innovation is one of the hottest topics in business—why leading magazines are full of articles about it, conference organizers are putting on $2,700-a-ticket conferences on it, and top-tier management consulting firms are building practices around it—this is a big part of the answer. In a world of forces that push toward the commoditization of everything, creating something new and different is the only way to survive. A product unlike any other can't be commoditized. A service that reaches deep into the psyche of the buyer can never be purchased solely on price. Creating such products and services was always valuable; now it's essential.

Yet fighting commoditization won't do much good if you don't keep it up. You can never stop because product life expectancies are getting drastically shorter. In the good old days, Wrigley produced the same three flavors of gum (Spearmint, Doublemint, and Juicy Fruit) for fifty-nine years and succeeded so grandly that William Wrigley built one of Chicago's great office buildings and bought Catalina Island, among other things. By contrast, consider the twenty-first-century saga of Wrigley's Chicago neighbor, Motorola—heroic and innovative pioneer of the cell phone at first, then scorned failure when it didn't jump fast enough to digital phones, then reborn champion when it created the sleek RAZR, then goat once again when it couldn't produce a successor, and finally a casualty of competition with its decision to unload its cell phone business completely. Motorola achieved lots of great cell phone innovations—just not enough of them.

As products and services live shorter lives, so do the business models of the companies that sell them. Time was when you could turn the crank on a good business model for thirty or forty years, and sometimes much longer; the regulated-utility model of AT&T and electricity companies worked for close to a hundred years. But now we hear the startling sound of CEOs admitting publicly that their business models don't work anymore. Paul Allaire said it out loud when he was CEO of Xerox; Michael Armstrong said it at AT&T; Bill Ford said it at Ford. Now companies with the most vaunted and successful business models of all time are being forced to change them. Southwest Airlines built itself into America's most valuable airline with a low-fare model that gave no special perks to business travelers; then results began to sag, and now it's offering special deals to exactly those customers. Dell became the world's largest PC maker with a model that sold directly, and only directly, to end users; then Hewlett-Packard surged ahead, and now Dell sells through Best Buy and other retailers. Adrian Slywotzky, an author and consultant who has worked with America's biggest companies for thirty years, has said that many companies now have to create innovative new business models every three or four years—"eight to ten years is heaven today."

Creativity and innovation may even be the key to the future economic prosperity of America and other developed countries, at least according to one line of thinking. The theory, though somewhat radical, resonates with various trends. It's radical because for three hundred years the source of economic dominance has clearly been leadership in science and technology; the countries or regions that were most advanced technologically have also been the most prosperous. But now a number of analysts, including Daniel H. Pink, author of *A Whole New Mind: Why Right-Brainers Will Rule the Future,* and Virginia Postrel, author of *The Substance of Style: How the Rise of Aesthetic Value Is Remaking Commerce, Culture, and Consciousness,* argue that this era may be ending. Technology will become commoditized by China and India, they say, being dispersed and adopted almost instantly after it's created. Economic value will arise instead from the powers of the right brain—creativity, imagination, empathy, aesthetics.

Exhibit A in their evidence is the Apple iPod. Apple didn't invent the MP3 music player; several models had been around for a few years before anyone had heard of the iPod, but they had never gone anywhere. Apple took an existing product and gave it an elegant design, created a simple, intuitive user interface, then added the business innovation of the iTunes Music Store, and somehow imbued the whole package with coolness. The result is 75 percent market share in music players and online music sales, a reordering of the music industry, and a multibillion-dollar boost to Apple's market value. The key wasn't technology. It was creativity, design, and a deep empathy with the customer.

In a different industry, how does Target thrive as a discount retailer against the massive power of Wal-Mart, a company more than five times its size that commands by far the world's most advanced retail computer systems? In part it does so by arranging for some of the world's top designers, such as Michael Graves and Isabelle de Borchgrave, to design some of the home's most pedestrian products, such as teakettles and breadbaskets, and then selling them in massive volume at discount prices. Following that strategy, Target can never be commoditized.

The phenomenon is sufficiently widespread that the MFA degree— master of fine arts—is gaining ground on the MBA as the preferred graduate degree for young people who want to make their mark in business. New York University has even begun offering a joint MBA/MFA degree.

Creativity and innovation have always been important; what's new is that they're becoming economically more valuable by the day. The issue, then, is how individuals and organizations can best respond. To help them, all those consultants, conferences, books, and magazines have coalesced into a vast innovation industry that offers virtually in-finite advice and guidance. Our task is not to inspect it all—impossible and fruitless—but rather to see if the principles of great performance provide any deep insight into the nature of creativity and innovation that would be useful to anyone trying to grow on these dimensions. They do, and these insights are especially valuable because, as with great performance generally, they run counter to many people's deeply held beliefs.

What We Think We Know

Two views in particular characterize what most of us "know that just ain't so" about innovation and creativity. One is that creative ideas come to us in the way a famous one came to Archimedes, in a eureka moment when everything suddenly becomes clear. It makes sense that we be-lieve this, because history as we learn it in school is filled with such stories. Often they're unforgettable. Archimedes running through the streets naked, having just settled into his bath and realizing he could measure the volume of an irregular object by water displacement, is an image no schoolchild will forget. Similarly, we see Abraham Lincoln on the train to Gettysburg, writing in a burst of inspiration one of the most eloquent speeches in American history. Or we picture Samuel Taylor Coleridge, who by his own account awoke from an opium-induced sleep to find "two to three hundred lines" of *Kubla Khan* standing fully formed before him in his mind. Great creators seem time and again to be struck by lightning bolts that reveal what no one else had seen or thought or imagined before.

The other thing we all think we know about creativity is that it can be inhibited by too much knowledge. We often say that someone is "too close to the problem" to see a solution. The broader principle is that if you know too much about a situation, a business, a field of study, then you can't have the flash of insight that is available only to someone unburdened by a lifetime of immersion in the domain. Edward de Bono, the best known business consultant on creative thinking, has stated this view explicitly: "Too much experience within a field may restrict creativity because you know so well how things *should be done* that you are unable to escape to come up with new ideas."

Again, we have good reasons for believing this. We've seen it confirmed at the organizational level countless times. Why didn't Western Union invent the telephone? Why didn't U.S. Steel invent the minimill? Why didn't IBM invent the personal computer? Over and over, the organizations that knew all there was to know about a technology or an industry failed to make the creative breakthroughs that would transform the business.

At the individual level the story is similar. Dean Keith Simonton, a professor at the University of California at Davis, conducted a large-scale study of more than three hundred creative high achievers born between 1450 and 1850—Leonardo da Vinci, Galileo, Beethoven, Rembrandt, for example. He determined the amount of formal education each had received and measured each one's level of eminence by the spaces devoted to them in an array of reference works. He found that the relation between education and eminence, when plotted on a graph, looked like an inverted *U:* The most eminent creators were those who had received a moderate amount of education, equal to about the middle of college. Less education than that—or more—corresponded to reduced eminence for creativity.

Other research seems to confirm de Bono's view. In a famous series of experiments first conducted more than sixty years ago, Abraham and Edith Luchins gave their subjects the task of measuring certain amounts of water using a set of different-sized jugs; for example, the jugs might hold 127 units, 21 units, and 3 units, and the task might be to measure out 100 units precisely. The subjects learned a set routine that worked for solving the first several measurement tasks they were given. When they were then given a measurement task that could be done using their learned routine or a much simpler one, they consistently failed to see the simpler one. And when they were given a task that could be done only with a simple but new routine, they failed to see it, and instead just kept trying to apply their known routine. Subjects who had never learned the original routine, however, saw the simple solution easily.

These concepts have permeated our views on creativity and in most of us have helped form those two core beliefs: Inspiration will strike when it's good and ready, whenever that may be; and if you want a creative solution to a problem, you'd better find someone who knows a little about the situation but not too much. Those beliefs, though they seem to be supported by evidence, will steer us wrong. They direct us away from the creating and innovating that we're capable of. The evidence underlying the principles of deliberate practice and great performance shows that in finding creative solutions to problems, knowledge—the more the better—is your friend, not your enemy. And it shows that creativity isn't a lightning bolt.

Know More, Innovate More

The greatest innovators in a wide range of fields—business, science, painting, music—all have at least one characteristic in common: They spent many years in intensive preparation before making any kind of creative breakthrough. Creative achievement never came suddenly, even in those cases in which the creator later claimed that it did. Whether it was the transistor or the Beatles' *Sgt. Pepper* album or the cell phone or Picasso's *Les Demoiselles d'Avignon,* it always followed a long earlier period of extremely hard work, and in most cases the creative products themselves were developed over a significant period. Great innovations are roses that bloom after long and careful cultivation.

The evidence is strikingly consistent. A study of seventy-six composers from many historical periods looked at when they produced their first notable works or masterworks, designations that were based on the number of recordings available. The researcher, Professor John R. Hayes of Carnegie Mellon University, identified more than five hundred works. As Professor Robert W. Weisberg of Temple University summarized the findings: "Of these works, only three were composed before year ten of the composer's career, and those three works were composed in years eight and nine." During those first ten or so years, these creators weren't creating much of anything that the outside world noticed. Professor Hayes termed the long and absolutely typical preparatory period "ten years of silence," which seemed to be required before anything worthwhile could be produced.

In a similar study of 131 painters, he found the same pattern. The preparation period was shorter—six years—but still substantial and seemingly impossible to defy, even for supposed prodigies like Picasso. A study of sixty-six poets found a few who produced notable works in less than ten years, but none who managed it in less than five; fifty-five of the sixty-six needed ten years or more.

These findings remind us strongly of the ten-year rule that researchers have found when they study outstanding performers in any domain. Other researchers, who weren't necessarily looking for evidence of this rule, have found it anyway. Professor Howard Gardner of Harvard wrote a book-length study (*Creating Minds*) of seven of the greatest innovators of the early twentieth century: Albert Einstein, T. S. Eliot, Sigmund Freud, Mahatma Gandhi, Martha Graham, Pablo Picasso, and Igor Stravinsky. A more diverse group of subjects would be hard to imagine, and Gardner did not set out to prove or disprove anything about the amount of work required for their achievements. But in summing up, he wrote, "I have been struck throughout this study by the operation of the ten-year rule. . . . Should one begin at age four, like Picasso, one can be a master by the teenage years; composers like Stravinsky and dancers like Graham, who did not begin their creative endeavors until later adolescence, did not hit their stride until their late twenties."

Not even the Beatles could escape the requirements of deep and broad preparation before producing important innovations. Professor Weisberg of Temple has studied the group's career and found that they spent thousands of hours performing together—sessions that closely matched the description of deliberate practice—before the world ever heard of them. In the early days they performed very few of their own songs, and those songs were undistinguished; we would never have known about them if they hadn't been dug up long after the group became successful. The group's first number 1 hit was "Please Please Me" (1963), written by John Lennon and Paul McCartney after they had been working together for five and a half years. One could certainly debate what kind of creative achievement that song represented; successful as it was, it was by no means a significant innovation in popular music. That had to wait until the group's so-called middle period, when they produced their albums *Rubber Soul, Revolver,* and *Sgt. Pepper's Lonely Hearts Club Band.* Those albums, consisting entirely of original music, transformed the domain. By the time of *Sgt. Pepper,* Lennon and McCartney had been working together—extremely hard—for ten years.

As for what exactly is going on during those long periods of preparation, it looks a lot like the acquisition of domain knowledge that takes place during deliberate practice. It is certainly intensive and deep immersion in the domain, frequently under the direction of a teacher, but even when not, the innovator seems driven to learn as much as possible about the domain, to improve, to drive himself or herself beyond personal limits and eventually beyond the limits of the field. Gardner looked back on the stories of the seven great innovators he studied and saw so many common themes that he combined them into a story of a composite character, whom he dubbed Exemplary Creator, or E.C. At some point in adolescence or early adult life, "E.C. has already invested a decade of work in the mastery of the domain and is near the forefront;

she has little in addition to learn from her family and from local experts, and she feels a quickened impulse to test herself against the other lead ing young people in the domain." As a result, "E.C. ventures toward the city that is seen as a center of vital activities for her domain."

We see some elements of deliberate practice apparent here: the large investment in mastering the domain, the quest for more advanced instruction, the constant pushing past the comfort zone. As that constant pushing continues, eventually "E.C. discovers a problem area or realm of special interest, one that promises to take the domain into uncharted waters." That journey can never be easy, and so here we see further parallels with great performers in other realms: "E.C. works nearly all the time, making tremendous demands on herself and on others, constantly raising the ante. In William Butler Yeats's formation, she chooses perfection of the work over perfection of the life." We have seen these extremely demanding regimes before, whenever we have looked at how deliberate practice has produced great performance.

Those examples largely from aesthetic fields are highly relevant for business because many of the most important business innovations in today's world are right-brain, aesthetic creations. Many other vital business innovations are in the realm of science, and here the notion that too much knowledge may interfere with innovation is even harder to support. Consider, for example, one of the most celebrated instances of creative problem solving in all of twentieth-century science, James Watson's and Francis Crick's discovery of the structure of DNA. Professor Weisberg, in a detailed study, has shown that several other distinguished scientists—including one, Linus Pauling, who would go on to win a Nobel Prize for other work—were trying to solve the same problem at the same time, each from a different perspective. If we presume that too much familiarity with a problem is a disadvantage, then we would expect to find that Watson and Crick came at this one unburdened by the excessive data that clouded the thinking of the other researchers. But in reality, the story was just the opposite. In those pre-

Internet days (the early 1950s), research findings were not disseminated nearly as easily as they are today, and Weisberg has shown how Watson and Crick came into possession of various papers, X-ray photographs, and raw data, as well as an understanding of X-ray crystallography and physics, that combined into a sum of critically important knowledge that none of the others possessed in total. Specifically, Watson and Crick had information leading them to deduce that the helix consisted of two strands (Pauling thought it was three), and that the strands were on the outside, with the "bases"—the steps in the spiral staircase—on the inside (some researchers thought the bases projected outward from the strands). They were able to calculate the pitch of the helix—the angle at which it spiraled—and how the bases connected to each other.

Watson and Crick were not the first to find each of these pieces of the puzzle. Other scientists realized earlier that the helix must be double, not single or triple, and two other teams beat Watson and Crick to the realization that the strands were on the outside of the molecule. Yet Watson and Crick were the first to solve the overall problem of DNA's structure because they, and they alone, had all the necessary facts. As Weisberg concludes, "one does not have to assume that Watson and Crick were different (or better) thinkers than the others. They simply had available what was needed to develop the correct model of DNA, and the others did not."

If we're looking for evidence that too much knowledge of the domain or familiarity with its problems might be a hindrance in creative achievement, we have not found it in the research. Instead, all evidence seems to point in the opposite direction. The most eminent creators are consistently those who have immersed themselves utterly in their chosen field, have devoted their lives to it, amassed tremendous knowledge of it, and continually pushed themselves to the front of it.

And what about evidence for the related notion that excessive schooling is correlated with lower creative achievement? The contradiction may amount to much less than it seems. Most obviously, years of school may not be a very good measure of domain knowledge, especially in certain realms. Someone with a Ph.D. in literature, for example, has acquired considerable knowledge about the history and interpretation of literature, usually of a specific type; but that's quite a different domain, requiring different knowledge and skills, from actually creating literature. Indeed, in many creative fields the person who pursues an advanced degree has consciously chosen a path that leads to a professorship, not to a life of innovating in that domain; it makes perfect sense that in these fields, those with the most years of formal schooling would be less eminent as innovators.

In science and technology the situation is different. Advanced education is absolutely required for creative problem solving in today's world; no one is going to cure cancer as a college sophomore. That's the reality of today, but remember that the study correlating higher education with lower creative eminence covered the period from 1450 to 1850. For the first half of that period, science as we know it scarcely existed; getting a high-level degree would not necessarily confer much scientific knowledge in an era when the fundamental principles of the scientific method were still unknown. For a research period that was in large part prescientific, it shouldn't be surprising that formal schooling and creative eminence in science didn't correlate. In short, in a wide range of fields, knowledge of the domain may bear little relation to years of schooling.

The bigger picture is that the great innovators aren't burdened by knowledge; they're nourished by it. And they acquire it through a process we've seen before, involving many years of demanding deliberate practice activities.

Innovation Doesn't Strike—It Grows

From here it's a short step to rethinking the popular view that great creative achievements are without precedent, that they spring "into sudden existence, like Minerva from the brain of Jupiter," as an admiring nineteenth-century author said of James Watt's steam engine. A closer look at notable innovations in business, the arts, and science (including Watt's steam engine) shows that they do not arise from nothingness; they are not even remotely unprecedented. Innovation doesn't reject the past; on the contrary, it relies heavily on the past and comes most readily to those who've mastered the domain as it exists.

Examples are everywhere, though none is more dramatic than Picasso's *Les Demoiselles d'Avignon,* deemed by art historians the most important painting of the twentieth century. Both Weisberg and Gardner, in their studies of creativity, consider it at length. It would be hard to name a creative work that seems more disconnected from anything that came before, with its grotesque inhuman faces on human bodies and aggressive nudity; in 1907, this was scandalous. Yet even this shocking creation was built up from many existing influences in art to which Picasso had been exposed—ancient Iberian sculpture, primitive art of Africa and the South Pacific, specific figures and compositions in paintings of Cézanne and Matisse. None of that diminishes the painting's power; but extensive research has shown that even this landmark work was not created out of nothing, as it may well seem, but was rather a brilliant new combination and elaboration of elements that had been developed over time and absorbed by an artist who had worked many years at mastering his field.

As in art, we also find this in science and technology, despite what we may occasionally have been taught in school. James Watt did not invent the steam engine, and what he did invent most certainly didn't spring into existence like Minerva from the brain of Jupiter. Many steam engines had been invented before Watt went to work in 1763, and several engines of the type invented by Thomas Newcomen were in commercial use in Britain, pumping water out of coal mines. Not that Newcomen invented the steam engine either; his device was an improvement on earlier machines, stretching back in a chain of developments such that no individual can be said to have invented the steam engine. The Newcomen engine wasn't very efficient, and Watt's design was much more efficient. It was also, of course, a giant innovation that through its role in the industrial revolution changed the course of history. But it was not some previously unimagined conception that burst forth like a miracle. Just the opposite: It came about because Watt was trying to improve on what already existed, the Newcomen engine, and his long training as a maker of scientific instruments gave him the skills and knowledge with which to do it.

Similarly, Eli Whitney didn't invent the cotton gin. Many machines had been developed to remove the seeds from cotton bolls, and they worked, but only with long-staple cotton, which wasn't economical to grow on a large scale. Whitney's device, using many of the same principles as existing machines, worked with short-staple cotton, and that made all the difference. Again, none of this diminishes the importance of the achievement; Whitney's machine revolutionized the economy of the American South and changed history. But it didn't appear out of nowhere; it was a brilliant improvement on existing designs that was possible only because Whitney understood what came before.

The steam engine and cotton gin were two of the most significant business innovations ever, and the stories of how such innovations come about remain the same up until the present. From the telegraph to the airplane to the Internet, they're all adaptations and extensions of what existed, made possible by great insights but entirely impossible without a deep knowledge of, and reliance on, past achievements. Less exalted innovations are no different. Inventor Jim Marggraff, who created the popular LeapPad electronic reading system for kids and the FLY computer pen, which digitizes and stores what you write, told the

New York Times that "each creation built on the work that went into making the previous one." In his experience, as in the experiences of other creators, innovations don't get easier to develop if you distance yourself from the problem. Instead, "the aha moments grow out of hours of thought and study," he said. Douglas K. van Duyne, an Internet entrepreneur who cofounded the Naviscent consulting firm, expressed the same view to the *Times:* "The idea of epiphany is a dreamer's paradise where people want to believe that things are easier than they are."

How Innovators Become Great

It's important to realize that innovation on the scale of the FLY computer pen, which may seem far removed from Beethoven's symphonies or Einstein's theories, is not fundamentally different in type. Until recently, researchers have often thought of creativity in two categories: Big-C creativity, which yields famous, influential products like the integrated circuit or *Huckleberry Finn;* and little-c creativity, which produces everyday creations like a TV commercial or a florist's arrangement of flowers. But Ronald A. Beghetto of the University of Oregon and James C. Kaufman of California State University at San Bernardino have suggested that both types of innovation exist "on the same developmental continuum," and that the continuum extends even further back than little-c creativity, to what they call mini-c creativity. In this framework, "all levels of creative performance follow a trajectory that starts with novel and personally meaningful interpretations (mini-c), which can then progress to interpersonally judged novel and meaningful contributions (little-c) and even develop into superior creative performance (Big-C)."

This perspective is highly significant because it ties together the evidence showing that creative achievement is attained in the same way as other kinds of achievement. As Beghetto and Kaufman state, "Big-C performance is more likely influenced by intense deliberate practice within a particular domain than by some special, genetic endowment of a few individuals." As creativity scholars, they see the work of Ericsson and his colleagues as providing "compelling empirical evidence in support of this developmental perspective, demonstrating the important role that deliberate practice plays in superior creative performance."

That is, innovators become great in the same way that everybody else does.

Yet we still face those research studies showing how people get stuck in ruts when they deal repeatedly with the same kinds of problems. How can these be squared with the experiences of real-world innovators that we've seen? An answer emerges when we look more closely at the research. In the famous water-jar experiments, subjects in a laboratory setting were given jars and a series of five problems, each of which could be solved by the same routine of filling and transferring in a certain way. They were then given a group of different problems, one of which could be solved only by a simpler procedure, which the subjects were unable to see. That result seemed to show that too much familiarity with a problem blinds a person to innovative solutions.

But if we step back and consider this situation, we see how different it is from the cases of actual creative problem solvers. These research subjects had not devoted themselves to the study of this domain or spent thousands of hours understanding problems of this type; as far as we can tell, everything they knew about this field was what they learned from the five same-solution problems contrived by the researchers and presented to them. If it then turns out that the subjects weren't very good at devising solutions to other, different problems, we should not be surprised; we certainly shouldn't suppose that this result tells us much about the factors that help or hinder eminent innovators. These experiments have been interpreted as showing what happens when people become too immersed in solving problems of a particular type, but they could be interpreted perhaps more plausibly, even compellingly, as showing what happens when people have not immersed themselves in their field of problem solving nearly enough. The experiments showed that subjects with no previous exposure to the problems were able to find a simple solution that the experienced subjects couldn't see, but the experiments didn't involve subjects who would be of most interest to us—those who had devoted major time and study to the problems. The research studies are interesting and justly famous, but they don't contradict what we've seen in the experiences of great creators and innovators.

And what about those legends of great creative products appearing suddenly and fully formed before their creators? The answer is simple: They aren't true. Coleridge may have been as good a public relations man as he was a poet, or so believes one critic who says Coleridge made up the dream story to help sell the poem. In any case, an earlier version of the poem has been found, showing that Coleridge revised it considerably before publication. Even in Coleridge's own version of the events, he says he faded into opium-induced slumber while reading a seventeenth-century book called *Pilgrimage,* then woke to see his famous poem that begins "In Xanadu did Kubla Khan / A stately pleasure-dome decree . . ." As the critic John Lowes discovered, *Pilgrimage* describes Khan's city in a passage that begins, "In Xamdu did Cublai Can build a stately Palace . . ." Coleridge, like all great creators, built on an existing foundation.

Abraham Lincoln's pen did not trace out the immortal words of the Gettysburg Address on the back of an envelope while he was riding to the battlefield; a number of drafts of the speech, on White House writing paper, have been found. As for the original eureka moment, nothing in Archimedes' extensive writings, or in the writings of any of his contemporaries, supports or even hints at the bathtub story. Scholars have concluded that it's a myth.

Making Organizations Innovative

Just as the principles that produce exceptional creativity and innovation in individuals are the same as the principles that produce great performance in general, the lessons are the same for organizations. All the steps described in the last chapter for helping organizations improve their performance will help them become more innovative as well. In addition, organizations can observe a few other principles that will specifically improve their chances of producing valuable innovations. The vast innovation industry has produced countless books on organizational creativity; but with the principles of deliberate practice and great performance in mind, a few ideas stand out.

The impression that emerges most strongly from the research on great creators is that of their enthusiastic immersion in their domain and their resulting deep knowledge of it. Since organizations are not innovative—only people are innovative—it follows that the most effective steps an organization can take to build innovation will include helping people expand and deepen their knowledge of their field. In the previous chapter we saw some of the ways an organization can do this. An additional approach, identified by McKinsey, is creating innovation networks within the organization—finding ways to connect people so that they can talk with one another about the problems they're working on, the approaches they're trying, and what they're learning. The rationale, as explained by McKinsey's Joanna Barsh, Marla M. Capozzi, and Jonathan Davidson, is that "Since new ideas seem to spur more new ideas, networks generate a cycle of innovation." We've seen that exceptional creators often build these networks on their own, a pattern observed by Howard Gardner, which he indicates when he notes that his Exemplary Creator moves to the big city in order to be among the leading figures of her domain.

One of the main reasons why the people in organizations don't produce more innovation is that the culture isn't friendly to it. New ideas aren't really welcomed. Risk taking isn't embraced. Corporate surveys show this, but we don't need the surveys; we all know it from experience. A revealing finding from McKinsey research explains why the problem doesn't get fixed very often: Top management doesn't think it's a problem. In a survey of six hundred executives, those at the top thought the main reason why their company wasn't more innovative was that it didn't have enough of the right people. Lower-level managers held a markedly different view—that the company had the right people, but the culture kept them from innovating as they should. Anyone who has spent time in organizations knows which of those two groups is more likely to be right. Changing an organizational culture to be friendlier to innovation, or in any other way, is a massive, long-term project that we can't explore in detail here, aside from making one observation: Culture change starts at the top. As long as those C-level executives think the culture is fine, it will never change. That's why McKinsey's survey explains a great deal about why so many companies aren't as innovative as they want to be.

Organizations can take two other steps that are especially effective in light of how innovation really happens: telling people what's needed, and giving them freedom to innovate.

Benjamin Zander, conductor of the Boston Philharmonic Orchestra, speaks often to business groups and typically takes them through a little exercise. He finds someone in the group whose birthday is that day, or the day before or after, and brings that person forward. Then he says to the group, "It's Mary's birthday! Sing her her song!" Without another word of instruction, the group immediately sings "Happy Birthday" to Mary. Then Zander says, "Well, that was very good. But you know what? I think you can do better. Now please sing it again, but this time—better. Go!" Complete silence. No one makes a sound. After several awkward seconds, Zander points out what has just happened: When everyone understood what to do, they did it easily, together, and without being led. But when they didn't understand—when told simply to sing it better—they became paralyzed.

It's often the same with innovation in organizations. Leaders exhort the troops to be innovative, but no one understands clearly what that means. Unsure where to go, they go nowhere. Organizations that want more innovation would benefit from telling everyone what kind of innovation would be most valuable. Because waiting for lightning bolts won't work—people would have to devote enormous time and effort to mastery of the field in which they hope to innovate—resources can be massively wasted if those people are pointed in the wrong direction. The right direction should be stated clearly: We need new ways to extend a product line, or new ways to expand in Latin America, or new ways to identify the needs of our customers, or new ways to lower our capital costs. What's important is that people understand the organization's priorities and thus know where innovation will do the most good.

The other step, giving people freedom to innovate, is a matter of motivation. The topic of why people put themselves through the rigors required for great performance is discussed in the last chapter, but it's worth noting here that on creative tasks in particular, some research suggests that people perform more innovatively when they are offered no extrinsic rewards; offering them a reward can actually reduce their creativity. Not all the research agrees, but the point is intuitively plausible: People who are internally driven to create do seem more creative than those who are just doing it for the money. As we've seen, money is never at the top of the list of motivators anyway, and when we're asking people to become masters of their field, we want to rely on the strongest possible inducements. That helps explain why some of the most notably innovative companies, such as 3M and Google, let employees spend a certain amount of their time, typically 10 to 20 percent, on any project that they find personally compelling. Such projects will not always help the company; that's a risk. But the benefit is that follow-your-heart policies embody a culture of trust, which is, as noted, an important contributor to creativity and almost impossibly difficult for many companies to adopt. That's why companies that adopt it hold a competitive advantage.

Understanding where innovation comes from is particularly important because we tend to believe deeply that this type of performance, even more than others, is a mysterious gift. It's easier for most of us to believe that a great tennis player achieved his success through the principles of deliberate practice than to believe that a great inventor got there that way. But the evidence shows that the most important factor in their high achievement is the same for both. Professor Raymond S. Nickerson of Tufts University has written that "the importance of domain-specific knowledge as a determinant of creativity is generally underestimated, even though investigators have given it considerable emphasis." What makes the biggest difference is the willingness to go through the demanding process of acquiring that knowledge over time. David N. Perkins of Harvard, surveying the many factors that have been proposed as important elements of creativity, wrote, "The clearest evidence of all demonstrates the connection between creative thinking and values broadly construed—a person's commitments and aspirations. . . . Much more than we usually suppose, creating is an intentional endeavor." Wanting to achieve mastery of a field, committing to the long, hard work of achieving it, and then intending to innovate—that's how it happens.

The heavy burden of the evidence is that creativity is much more available to us than we tend to think. The most significant constraint, as with all kinds of exceptional performance, is mostly likely to be our willingness to do the difficult work required. On that point, the study of innovation in particular has raised questions that are actually significant for all types of top performance: How early in life should the work of deliberate practice begin, and how late in life is it effective? In creative fields such as music, people may begin training when they're very young and keep working until they're very old. What is the larger meaning of this? Does achieving exceptional performance take longer than it used to? If so, what is the role of the supporting environment?

It turns out that the power of deliberate practice extends very broadly through life. We turn next to why that is so and what it implies.

Chapter Ten

Great Performance in Youth and Age

The extraordinary benefits of starting early
and continuing on and on

Why are Nobel Prize winners receiving their awards at increasingly advanced ages? They are, and at a fairly dramatic rate.

The explanation reveals a number of trends and basic realities about exceptional performance. It shows why reaching the highest levels in many fields is harder than it used to be. That fact forces us to examine the effectiveness of deliberate practice throughout life, from the earliest ages to the oldest. It also leads us to consider the kinds of support structures that will be needed to help anyone reach exceptional achievements in the future—for one of the most consistent findings in the research is that nobody makes this journey alone.

The advancing ages of Nobel laureates and other innovators was discovered by Benjamin F. Jones of the Kellogg School of Management at Northwestern University. He examined the winners of Nobel Prizes in the sciences and economics as well as others who had made the most notable advances in science and technology over a period that was roughly the twentieth century. When he determined the ages at which they had made their outstanding advances, he found a surprising fact: The average age had increased by about six years during just a one-hundred-year period. The finding survived every test of statistical significance. Something big was going on, but why?

The most obvious explanation would be that average life spans increased greatly over the twentieth century, so this finding makes perfect sense. Of course Nobel laureates were getting older; so was everybody else. The trouble is, this explanation doesn't hold up. Scientists and economists very rarely make important contributions in their later years, so it doesn't matter that they might be living to eighty rather than sixty-five. In addition, confirming this logic, Jones was able to use sophisticated statistical techniques to control for the aging population, and he found that its effect was zero.

The real explanation was at the other end of the spectrum. These eminent innovators were getting older not because the oldest ones were pulling the average up, but because the youngest ones were pushing the average up. Einstein won the Nobel Prize in physics for work he did at age twenty-six, and no one thought that was remarkable. Quite the contrary. Paul Dirac, who also won a Nobel Prize in physics for work he did at age twenty-six (in 1928), wrote a famous verse on exactly this point: "Age is, of course, a fever chill/ that every physicist must fear./ He's better dead than living still/ when once he's past his thirtieth year."

Yet by the century's end, any physicist who died before the age of thirty would probably remain unheard of. Jones found that the innovators he studied began making active contributions to their fields at age twenty-three, on average, in 1900, but by 1999 the average age had risen to thirty-one, a very large increase of eight years, and of course the ages at which they made their greatest contributions were even later. The reason Nobel laureates and other innovators are getting older is not that they're living longer but that it's taking them significantly longer to make a contribution in the first place.

Other research shows that this trend applies not just to the most advanced thinkers. The age at which people receive their first patent, across a wide range of fields in business and government, has been increasing at a rate of six to seven years per century. Jones concluded, "Taking the facts together, we see similar trends among both the greatest minds and ordinary inventors. We appear to be seeing a general phenomenon."

It's general because it's happening in all heavily knowledge-based fields, including those in which many people work. Knowledge is the foundation of great performance, and in fields where important advances are being made continually, mastering the accumulated knowledge takes longer all the time. That's easy to see in physics. When you think of all the twentieth-century giants in this field—Planck, Bohr, Heisenberg, Fermi, Feynman, and many others—it's clear why today's aspiring physicist needs many more years of preparatory study than even Einstein did.

But the same principle holds beyond physics and the other hard sciences, extending into all knowledge-rich realms, emphatically including business. Economics and corporate finance have been transformed in the past hundred years. Marketing, operations research, organizational behavior—all have developed into advanced disciplines that require far more study than in the past. Even the ever-swelling U.S. tax code—now four times longer than *War and Peace*—demands many years of devoted study by those whose work requires that they understand it. The Nobel Prize effect is happening in all these domains and many more.

Reinforcing that effect are generally rising standards, which are forcing more intensive preparation on anyone who hopes to excel. We saw in chapter 1 how several factors are pushing standards up in virtually every domain as competition increases and methods of advancement are constantly improved. And not just in the world of work: All parents with kids applying to college seem to be extremely glad that they applied back when they did, and not today.

The Supporting Environment

As the demands of excellence increase in every field, so grows the importance of the supporting environment in which prospective achievers dwell, starting at the earliest age. No one becomes extraordinary on his or her own, and a striking feature in the lives of great performers is the valuable support they received at critical times in their development. Certainly some great performers have had to fight poverty and discouragement, but that's not the same as lack of support. In virtually every case, the supporting environment is critical.

It exists at several levels, some of which you can't do much about—though the findings on supporting environments at every level furnish insight that's valuable in shaping environments that you can control. Dean Keith Simonton has observed that "expertise of the highest order is most likely to appear in a particular sociocultural context." For example, Kenneth Clarke, the famous English art critic and author of *Civilization,* believed that great art was usually created amid stability; you won't get many great statues or symphonies from residents of a city under siege. Simonton's research found that "exceptional creators are less likely to develop during times of anarchy but are more likely to develop during periods of political fragmentation, when a civilization is divided into numerous independent states," which is a pretty good description of Renaissance Italy. Cultures encourage or discourage specific pursuits at different times. In Western cultures today you'll get plenty of support for medical research into a cure for cancer, but two hundred years ago phony cancer cures were so prevalent that you would have been regarded as a dangerous charlatan.

If the culture is at one end of the spectrum of supporting environments—the widest, most immutable part—then at the other end is the home, and wide research suggests that it is by far the most important part. The circumstances in which people begin developing in their eventual field of achievement can make a major difference, and even in business and other domains where development often begins later than childhood, findings about effective supporting environments in the home hold larger lessons that can be applied more generally.

The greatest value of a supporting home environment is that it enables a person to start developing early. We've seen that in a few specialized fields, such as baseball pitching and ballet, the body can be adapted in critical ways only at early ages, after which the bones calcify and the changes become impossible; the pitcher will never get his arm back and the dancer will never turn her feet out as fully as necessary. Brain adaptations seem to follow a similar pattern in at least a few cases. Violinists' brains devote more territory to the workings of the left hand—the one that plays the notes—than do other people's brains, and also more space than is devoted to the workings of their own right hands, with the effect much more pronounced in people who started their music study at an early age. A separate effect involves myelin, the substance that wraps slowly around neurons with practice, insulating and strengthening key connections in the brain. Practice in childhood causes myelin to build up more than does practice in adulthood. A study of professional pianists found that the more practice they did before age sixteen, the more myelin they had in the critical parts of their brains. Starting early holds advantages that become less available later in life.

Yet even more important than these advantages is a different factor, and that is the simple matter of time and resources. As we have seen repeatedly, becoming world-class great at anything seems to require thousands of hours of focused, deliberate practice. For example, the top-ranked violinists in the Berlin study had accumulated about ten thousand hours of practice by age twenty, at which point they were practicing some twenty-eight hours a week and spending many additional hours studying, taking lessons, preparing, and organizing. For an adult facing the responsibilities of a family and a career, devoting that kind of time to purely developmental activities—activities that cost money rather than earn money—would be exceedingly tough. Only in childhood and adolescence will the time typically be available.

That reality creates another advantage to starting early, a competitive one that we've considered before. In any field where people can start early, starting late may put one in an eternal and possibly hopeless quest to catch up. For example, when those top-ranked violinists turn professional, they don't stop practicing. On the contrary, they practice even more, averaging more than thirty hours a week, accumulating more than fifteen hundred hours a year. Any adult thinking of starting a professional career in any field in which some participants begin their development as small children should first get out a calculator and face the music.

What Homes Can Teach Organizations

The specific nature of the supporting environment is obviously crucial, and a number of researchers have identified the most important characteristics. In the largest and most famous examination of the topic, the legendary educational researcher Benjamin S. Bloom directed a study of 120 young men and women who were among America's top performers in widely divergent fields—piano playing, sculpting, swimming, tennis, mathematics, and neurology. After extensive interviews with the performers and their families, his team found that their home environments shared a number of traits.

Despite wide variations in the parents' backgrounds, professions, and incomes, their homes tended to be child-oriented. Kids were important, and the parents were willing to do a lot—almost anything—to help them. The parents also believed in and modeled a strong work ethic. Work came before play, obligations had to be met, goals were to be pursued. In one of the most cited conclusions from Bloom's report, he found that "To *excel,* to *do one's best,* to *work hard,* and to *spend one's time constructively* were emphasized over and over again." In an organization, this would be called the culture—the norms and expectations that are simply in the air.

The parents of these high achievers gave them strong guidance on the general choice of a field, but chance played a large role in the specific choice. The artists tended to come from artistic parents, the athletes from athletic parents, the mathematicians and neurologists from very learned parents, and the parents provided early encouragement in those directions. But a child might end up studying the piano because a piano was available, or become a swimmer because the swimming team needed one more member. The children were not irresistibly drawn to specific fields, nor did their parents force them.

The parents did choose teachers, which was one of their most important roles as their children progressed and needed to be challenged at higher levels. The child's initial teacher was almost always someone who happened to be convenient—a local coach, teacher, or relative. But invariably these kids progressed to a level where they needed a better teacher, and these next teachers were frequently not convenient; parents had to devote lots of time and energy to finding the right teacher and then driving the child to and from lessons. Ultimately these young achievers moved on to some form of master-level teacher, a step that demands major sacrifices of time, money, and energy by both parents and students.

In an organization this progression is analogous to choosing developmental assignments that continually stretch an employee's abilities. Employees aren't children, but many of them, like children, will not voluntarily keep seeking new work experiences that stress their weakest professional muscles; the temptation to continue doing what you do comfortably is too great. Employers, like parents and coaches, have to keep pushing them to develop, and the lesson for employers is that the process requires sacrifices on their part as well—in the form of suboptimal performance by a business unit when a manager is taken away from it for a developmental assignment elsewhere, or periods of little or no productivity from an employee while he or she is learning new skills. But the lesson also is that these sacrifices pay off.

In addition to choosing appropriate new teachers, the parents in the research project monitored their children's practice, made sure there was time for it, and made sure they did it. This is worth a closer look not only because practice is centrally important to achievement but also because kids in particular seem to hate it. If the research suggests factors that contribute to kids practicing, those findings may be valuable to everyone. Mihaly Csikszentmihalyi of the University of Chicago and colleagues investigated why it's easier for some adolescents than others to sustain concentrated, effortful study, the core of deliberate practice and high achievement. The research focused on the students' family environments, evaluating them on two dimensions, stimulation and support. A stimulating environment was one with lots of opportunities to learn and high academic expectations. A supportive environment was one with well-defined rules and jobs, without much arguing over who had to do what, and in which family members could rely on one another. The researchers classified family environments as stimulating or not and supportive or not, creating four possible combinations. Adolescents living in three of those combinations reported the typical low-interest, low-energy experience of studying. But in the fourth combination, the environment that was both stimulating and supportive, students were much more engaged, attentive, and alert in their studying.

This key finding fits exactly with observations in Bloom's research. The environments he examined were also stimulating—"parents encouraged the *curiosity* of their children at an early age and answered their questions with great care"—and were structured and supportive, with everyone having clear roles and tasks, and parents going to some lengths to support their children's practice. In this light we see another clue to why so few organizations produce a steady flow of top performers. Most organizations are not intellectually stimulating, even when the field itself might seem fascinating; rather than offering opportunities to learn and rewarding curiosity, the typical organization leaves inquisitive employees to find their own ways to learn. And instead of furnishing structure and support—meaning clear roles and responsi-

bilities in a positive, forward-looking, build-on-successes environment—
many organizations operate in a cover-your-ass culture that is mainly
about avoiding blame. Such cultures have always seemed like a miserable fact of life, but the research on supporting environments shows
specifically why they're poisonous. It shows additionally why any organization that can buck the trends by providing stimulation, structure,
and support is not only rare but also powerful.

Should We Create Business Prodigies?

We've seen often that early training can produce high achievers who
are surprisingly young, and the research has shown us how that happens. We've grown accustomed to watching sixteen-year-old pianists,
chess players, and gymnasts who are astoundingly good. Yet why is it
that in certain other fields, notably business, we never see sixteen-year-
old wonders? The glib answer is that a kid of that age can't legally sign
a check or a lease; in fact that answer embodies larger truths about
when to begin training a young person in particular domains, how to
do it, and what the principles of early development mean for business
and related fields.

The fundamental reason why there are no teenage prodigies in certain domains is that it's impossible to accumulate enough development
time by the teenage years. Sometimes the reason is simply physical size.
A five-year-old can practice the piano or violin—reduced-size violins
are made for that purpose—but cannot practice the trombone or double
bass because they're just too big. So world-class trombonists and
double-bassists tend to be older. In other cases a decade of development
is not enough. This is the Nobel Prize effect: There are no teenage particle physicists, even though a child can start learning math and science
at age five, because acquiring the necessary knowledge these days seems
to take at least twenty years.

Is that why we don't see eighteen-year-old business wizards—

because the sheer volume of necessary knowledge is too great to be acquired by that age? The explanation doesn't seem completely persuasive. Let's leave aside those businesspeople who are actually scientists on the payroll of a corporation, and focus on managers. The knowledge and skills needed to be a successful manager are formidable for sure. On the other hand, as any manager who's being frank will tell you, running a business is frequently not rocket science. Formulating a business unit strategy is a lot of work, but not work on the order of, say, proving Fermat's Last Theorem (which took 357 years).

The answer may instead be that traditionally, training in business skills doesn't start early. Our discussion of early development will have caused any businessperson to reflect that virtually nothing like this happens in business—there isn't intensive, focused development of business skills in young people that's anything like what happens with swimmers, artists, and mathematicians, for example. The question then arises of whether it's even possible. Postponing for a moment the issue of whether it's desirable, would it be possible and effective to train young people intensively in business knowledge and skills?

The answer is clearly yes. Development must always begin at the beginning, so you wouldn't try teaching a five-year-old about the capital asset pricing model or the inner workings of the Food and Drug Administration. But you could start teaching basic domain knowledge— the facts of a specific business—and of course this was done routinely for centuries until fairly recently. Kids started learning the family business or some other business before age ten. We can appreciate the wisdom of the apprenticeship system, which immersed people in a particular field under a skilled teacher's direction from a young age, in keeping with the basic principles of early development.

Beyond general domain knowledge, it would be possible to train quite young people in more specific business skills. Basic finance concepts would fit perfectly well in an elementary-level math curriculum; just ask Ram Charan, one of the world's most eminent management consultants, who says his deep feel for corporate finance began with what he learned in his family's shoe shop in India, where he worked from the age of eight. Larry Bossidy, former CEO of Honeywell and one of the most celebrated CEOs of recent decades, will tell you something similar about his childhood experiences in his own family's shoe shop in Pittsfield, Massachusetts. Fairly young children could also be educated in the business aspects of probability and statistics, which are extraordinarily important in making good economic decisions and avoiding the irrational errors that people very commonly commit, as the study of behavioral finance has revealed. Corporations' number-one complaint about new young employees is that they're terrible at writing and speaking; training them in those skills from a business perspective could begin at a very early age. From such beginning steps, it would seem possible to train young people several hours a day over a period of many years for high achievement in a specific business.

It would be possible—but would it be good? Should we use the principles of great performance and early development to turn out little Jack Welches and Donald Trumps prepared to be corporate titans by the time they reach voting age? The evidence suggests we could do it, or at least come close, yet most of us instinctively reject that idea. Why? The instinct is worth examining.

Developed countries don't use the apprenticeship system anymore because in the nineteenth century the nature of work changed. Most Americans back then got no more than an eighth-grade education, which was all you needed to work on a farm, and that's what most people did. But as the industrial revolution made farming more efficient—thus requiring fewer people—and sparked the growth of factories, which needed more people, eighth-grade schooling was no longer enough. In the early twentieth century something called the high school movement swept America as towns nationwide decided that every student should complete twelve years of schooling. At first this was job training; the new high schools taught students basic math, English, and science skills, and sometimes much more specific skills as well, that would equip them for the growing industrial economy. But later, as the country got richer, high school curricula expanded beyond job skills into all corners of the liberal arts. More students went on to college, the great majority pursuing liberal arts majors. It became a mark of the developed world's twentieth-century prosperity—many would say one of its proudest achievements—that a full, rounded, advanced education came within reach of almost everyone. Your work and daily life might never require you to know Homer or Shakespeare or the history of Russia, or, for that matter, trigonometry or chemistry. But there's more to life than work, and knowing these things enriches your life and makes you a more fulfilled person.

Seen from that perspective, the idea of adults deciding to sacrifice their child's broad education in order to put little Max or Ashley through hours of daily training to become a top-notch business executive by age twenty-one seems barbarous. And maybe it is. But as we think about it, let's keep a couple of points in mind.

First, our society has very little problem with kids being directed toward fields other than business at early ages. No one seems to think that Earl Woods was a bad father for directing Tiger emphatically toward golf from the age of eighteen months. On the contrary, he seems to have been a wonderful father, and his son adored him. Nor do we seem to mind when young achievers in other fields sacrifice a broad education in order to focus on their chosen domains. A bit of tut-tutting followed LeBron James's decision to go straight from high school to pro basketball, but now that he's enormously wealthy and popular, that's all forgotten. The Polgar sisters learned enough about nonchess subjects to pass the required exams, but they never went to school at all; nonetheless, the Hungarian public hailed them as national heroes. In these and other cases of high achievement at early ages, the brilliance of what has been achieved blots out any sight of what has been given up. If similar techniques were applied to early training in business, and similar results produced, would the same effect follow?

Second, even if we reject the notion of purposefully turning five-year-olds into future banking executives or textile plant managers or retail strategists, other societies may not hesitate. Fast-developing nations in Asia, Africa, and Latin America will view the research on early development from their own perspectives, and there's no reason to assume they'll be just like ours. If governments or families in some of these countries decide to focus on turning out managers who are whizzes at age twenty-one and will just keep getting better, we will have to confront that reality and perhaps think again about our own views.

Defying Age

Our look at how some people reach remarkable heights at early ages should not obscure an important fact about age and achievement: Even when young people perform exceptionally, they usually develop further. Yo-Yo Ma was a world-famous cellist at age twenty, but he was much better at forty. Jamie Dimon was an amazingly accomplished financial services executive at age twenty-nine, but he was much better at fifty, as CEO of JPMorgan Chase. The reality of continued improvement over many years has led researchers to study how great performers develop over their lifetimes. The findings illuminate how performance is—and isn't—affected by advancing age.

One of the best established and least surprising findings in psychology is that as we age, we slow down. Remembering things, solving unfamiliar problems—these take about twice as long in our sixties as they did in our twenties. We move more slowly. Coordinating our arms and legs is more difficult. We've all seen it happen, and anyone in their thirties or beyond has experienced it. So we might reasonably suppose that this unavoidable trend spells doom for excellent performance. If our minds and bodies deteriorate with the march of time, there would seem to be nothing we can do to maintain top-level performance beyond a certain number of years.

Thus it's surprising to find that this isn't true at all, and not just in a few notable cases, but generally. Somehow, excellent performers manage to continue achieving at high levels well beyond the point where age-related declines would seem to make that impossible.

Example: On January 10, 2008, the New York Philharmonic made an announcement that shocked those who were intimately familiar with the orchestra as well as those who knew nothing about it. The news was that Stanley Drucker, the Philharmonic's principal clarinetist, would retire after the 2008–2009 season. That surprised aficionados, because Drucker was such a fixture of the Philharmonic that it was hard to imagine the orchestra without him. But it surprised nonfans even more because it seemed impossible to believe: By the time of his retirement, Drucker would have been performing with the Philharmonic for sixty-one years. Possessing what must be one of the working population's shorter résumés, he joined the orchestra at age nineteen and would be retiring at eighty.

Cases of people working for the same employer for extremely long times are not rare, but this is different. How could anyone as old as Drucker possibly perform at the level required of the lead clarinetist in one of the world's preeminent orchestras? How could he move his fingers fast enough? How could he remember long clarinet concertos, which he continued to perform from memory as a soloist?

Research reveals an answer that applies across fields. Studies in a very broad range of domains—management, aircraft piloting, music, bridge, and others—show consistently that excellent performers suffer the same age-related declines in speed and general cognitive abilities as everyone else—except in their field of expertise. For example, a study of older expert pianists found that their general processing speed had declined just as their age would predict. Among the general population this decline is evident in many ways. Psychologists measure how fast people can push a button in response to a question on a screen or how fast they can tap their fingers or coordinate finger movements; all these things slow down with age. But while excellent pianists slowed down like everyone else in how fast they could respond to a choice on a screen, which is not a skill that makes much difference to a pianist, they didn't slow down at all when it came to piano-related skills like finger tapping or finger coordination. They could do those things as if they hadn't aged at all. It's the same story in many other fields. When it comes to tasks that are part of their domain of expertise, great performers can keep performing at a high level even after their skills outside their domain have deteriorated.

In light of what we've seen about the nature of great performance, this finding shouldn't be surprising. After all, we've seen repeatedly that great performance doesn't come from superior general abilities; it comes from specific skills that have been developed in a particular way over a long period of time. So it makes sense that when general abilities decline with age, that decline need not affect the specific skills that undergird great performance. It need not affect them—yet there must be more to the story, because of course there are plenty of great performers whose skills do indeed decline with age. For every Stanley Drucker, there are many others whose names we've forgotten, high-level performers in many fields who faded away after brief, successful careers. So why do some carry on, but not others?

The explanation seems to be the factor that made them excellent performers in the first place, deliberate practice. Just as mere experience, even decades of it, is not enough to make anyone a great performer, neither is it enough to defy the effects of age, even in a person's field of specialization. Several studies have shown that just continuing to work at a job is not enough to stave off age-related declines. Architects have presumably developed strong spatial abilities, for example, but in a study of architects who were not distinguished except by continued employment, those abilities declined predictably with age. It takes something more, and what it takes is effortful, focused, designed practice. Those expert pianists who maintained their piano skills as they aged were compared with a sample of amateur pianists, some of whom had forty years of experience but had long since given up anything that could be called deliberate practice. The amateurs, unlike the experts, suffered predictable, across-the-board age-related declines.

The reason deliberate practice works in this way is no mystery, for we've already seen the effect. In general, well-designed practice, pursued for enough time, enables a person to circumvent the limitations that would otherwise hold back his or her performance, and circumventing limitations is the key to high performance at an advanced age. In a study of excellent chess players, the older ones chose moves just as well as the younger ones, but they did it in a different way. They didn't consider as many possible moves because they couldn't, but they compensated through greater knowledge of positions.

More generally, continued deliberate practice enables top performers to maintain skills that would otherwise decline with age, and to develop other skills and strategies to compensate for declines that can no longer be avoided. That approach can work for a long time. The piano virtuoso Wilhelm Backhaus said that in his fifties he increased his practice of études, which he felt he needed in order to maintain his technical skills. At a later age, the pianist Arthur Rubinstein felt that he could no longer play as fast as he used to, but he developed a strategy for compensating: In the passages preceding the fast ones, he would slow down more than he used to, so the following passages, even though he played them slower than in the old days, would seem faster by contrast. He continued to perform publicly, to great acclaim, until he was eighty-nine.

Just as improved methods of practice have raised standards of performance in virtually every field over time, they are also enabling top performers to continue achieving at high levels for more years than previously thought possible. We see the effect dramatically in sports, where the average age of professional players has been edging up for years. In baseball, Julio Franco played for the Atlanta Braves in the 2007 season at age forty-nine, thanks to a regimen of intense exercise and carefully designed diet that's unlike anything that was used in baseball decades ago. His trainer told the *New York Times,* "When I got acquainted with him, I learned quickly that you can't associate him with people of his age. His discipline is unlike anything I've ever seen." Franco is by far the oldest player in major league baseball, and that's assuming you believe he was born in 1958, as his official bio states. Early bios said 1954, which would make him a fifty-three-year-old major league player.

Other sports have their Methuselahs. In pro football, Atlanta's Morten Andersen is forty-seven, and in pro basketball, Houston's Dikembe Mutombo is forty-two; each is at or near his sport's all-time-record age, and as of this writing, each is still playing. The same phenomenon is happening in amateur sports—running, swimming, and others. Researchers are finding many examples of runners who, through harder and better-designed training, maintain performance as they age at levels never previously matched, and even some who improve, running faster at sixty than they did at fifty. A seventy-four-year-old man in 2004 ran a marathon in 2:54:44, which is four minutes faster than the gold medal performance in the 1896 Olympics.

We can also train our mental abilities far later in life than previously believed. For decades the conventional view in medicine was that once we reach adulthood, we can only lose neurons, not add them, and our brain's ability to adapt itself to new challenges, known as brain plasticity, shuts down. More recent research shows that none of this is true. Our brains are perfectly able to add new neurons well into old age when conditions demand it, and brain plasticity doesn't stop with age. Give your brain the right kind of training—for example, by making it try to do two things at once—and plasticity will increase in the regions that normally show the greatest atrophy in later years.

A phenomenon like the aging of professional athletes may be occurring in purely cognitive fields as well. Certainly we're seeing businesspeople performing at the highest levels at advanced ages. Warren Buffett continues to run Berkshire Hathaway brilliantly in his late seventies. Rupert Murdoch, at about the same age, is aggressively expanding his huge media conglomerate, News Corporation. Henry Kissinger continues his work as a consultant in his mideighties, and Sumner Redstone continues to run Viacom and CBS at the same age. This is not merely an instance of life expectancies increasing generally; what's significant is that these executives and others are able to continue working effectively at the top echelons of business ten or twenty years past what used to be considered normal retirement.

Even Benjamin Jones's study of top scientific innovators may be worth updating. Recall his finding that the upper limit of their ages at the time of their innovations wasn't increasing; achievement fell off sharply after about age forty, and the average age of the whole group was about thirty-nine. His study period ended in 1999, but if one looks at Nobel Prize winners in physics since then, one finds a noticeably older group. Their average age at the time of their achievement was about forty-one, and in this discipline where Nobelist Paul Dirac thought a person was "better dead than living still" after age twenty-nine, we find among the twenty-two winners from 2000 through 2007 some who made their mark at ages fifty-eight, sixty-one, and sixty-five.

Our insight into how it's possible to maintain top-level performance into the later decades of life helps us understand those cases in which it doesn't happen. Most people stop the deliberate practice necessary to sustain their performance. We can't necessarily criticize them. It may be a completely rational decision, for example in the case of a pro athlete who has earned millions of dollars and has little to gain but much to lose, in the possibility of serious injury, by continuing to play.

Businesspeople who get rich early may see no further reason to keep challenging themselves.

More broadly, every high performer is continually making a cost-benefit analysis when it comes to deliberate practice, and as the years go by, the costs increase while the benefits diminish. Improving performance becomes more difficult, and the performer focuses more on just maintaining a given level; as even that become unrealistic, the performer seeks ways to compensate for the encroaching weaknesses. The hours required for all this remain punishing, and it's easy to understand how elite performers may come to feel the effort is no longer worth what it produces. The key concept, however, is that for many years in a person's life—more years than most of us believe—performance deterioration in our chosen field isn't an inexorable process. It is, rather, a choice about how much effort we want to invest in our performance. As Karl Malone, the NBA's second all-time top scorer, told the *Los Angeles Times* about aging athletes, "It's not that their bodies stop, it's just that they've decided to stop pushing it."

Eventually, of course, everyone's performance declines. Even the most diligent deliberate practice cannot fend off the advancing years forever. When Arthur Rubinstein gave up performing publicly at eighty-nine, it was because he was becoming blind and deaf. He couldn't practice his way past that. And then there's the ultimate slowing down, which even the greatest performers must confront. Warren Buffett told his shareholders in his 2008 letter, "I've reluctantly discarded the notion of my continuing to manage the portfolio after my death—abandoning my hope to give new meaning to the term 'thinking outside the box.'"

The perspectives of both youth and age raise a profound question about great performance, one we've touched on before but now must face directly. If it's all about the punishing demands of deliberate practice, the continual, painful pushing beyond what's comfortable, for hours a day and years on end, then why does anyone do it? A parent can make a child practice, but not with the focus and intensity needed to become great. Something else must make the child do that. At life's other extreme, Stanley Drucker doesn't need to work, and he certainly doesn't need to put in the hours required to remain the top clarinetist in one of the world's greatest orchestras. Warren Buffett doesn't need to work. Why do they push themselves? Why does a chess player study four or five hours a day when becoming even one of the world's top-ranked grand masters does not necessarily bring wealth? Why do some young businesspeople push themselves beyond their jobs' considerable daily demands to acquire more knowledge and skills when the payoff is uncertain and may be years away?

We know that great performance comes from deliberate practice, but deliberate practice is hard. It's so hard that no one can do it without the benefit of passion, a truly extraordinary drive. So we need to know where that originates.

Chapter Eleven

Where Does the Passion Come From?

Understanding the deepest question
about great performance

Consider what Shizuka Arakawa had been through by the time she won the gold medal in figure skating at the 2006 Winter Olympics in Turin, Italy. She was twenty-four and had been training as a skater since age five. Winning the gold requires flawless performance of moves that the rest of us would consider simply impossible; Arakawa's specialty was something called a layback Ina Bauer—bending backward almost double with the feet pointing in opposite directions—leading into a three-jump combination. Perfecting such moves requires huge quantities of practice, and falling down during much of it. For Arakawa it took nineteen years. A study of figure skaters found that sub-elite skaters spent lots of time working on the jumps they could already do, while skaters at the highest levels spent more time on the jumps they couldn't do, the kind that ultimately win Olympic medals and that involve lots of falling down before they're mastered.

Falling down in figure skating means landing on your behind, protected only by a thin costume, on hard, cold ice. A few moments with a calculator tell us that by an extremely conservative estimate, Arakawa's road to the gold medal involved at least twenty thousand derriere impacts on an unforgiving surface. But they paid off. The results included Olympic glory, national adoration, and the suddenly fashionable use of "Ina Bauer" as a vogue word throughout Japan.

Arakawa's story is not just impressive in itself but also valuable as a metaphor. Landing on your butt twenty thousand times is where great performance comes from. That fact raises the question of why anyone would go through it for a reward that is many years away. This is the deepest question in the study of exceptional performance. In a sense, it is infinitely deep. It's a question about what people decide to do with their lives and what kind of passion drives them. The answer may extend so far into a person's psyche that no one can get all the way there. It sometimes takes us beyond psychology and into psychiatry. But that doesn't mean the question is a black hole or that pursuing it is hopeless. On the contrary, many findings provide intriguing hints as to why great performers pay the price they must pay. The research also sheds light on how we can answer the question as it applies to ourselves.

Two Kinds of Drive

The central question about motivation to achieve great performance is whether it's intrinsic or extrinsic. Do people do it because they feel driven, or is it possible to induce them to do what it takes? Most of us believe the drive must be ultimately intrinsic, because we feel nothing could make someone endure the pain and sacrifice of deliberate practice for decades unless that person carried his or her own compulsion to do it. Much of the research supports this view. In particular, research on motivation in creativity has focused on the question of intrinsic versus extrinsic, and it's helpful and relevant for two reasons: In many fields creativity represents the highest level of excellent performance, where people go beyond anything already achieved and make new contributions; and creativity, like effective practice in any domain, requires intense focus and concentration, which is the element that's most demanding and difficult to sustain.

The consistent finding reported by many researchers examining many domains is that high creative achievement and intrinsic motivation go together. Creative people are focused on the task (How can I solve this problem?) and not on themselves (What will solving this problem do for me?). Young people who excel in science and math are more intrinsically motivated than their lower-performing peers. Scientists who make important discoveries are found to be passionately involved in their field. A wide range of creative achievers seem to be devoted to great questions or problems in their field—scientific, commercial, artistic—and feel driven to pursue them for decades.

Look at the issue from any perspective and the results seem to be the same. People who rank high for intrinsic motivation on various psychological tests consistently produce work that is judged more creative in studies. Conversely, people who work in professions demanding creativity (artists, research scientists) reliably rank higher on tests of intrinsic motivation.

The work of University of Chicago psychologist Mihaly Csikszentmihalyi suggests one specific mechanism (of many that might exist) that could link intrinsic motivation with the demands of deliberate practice. His famous work on "flow" describes a state in which a person is so totally involved in a task that time slows down, enjoyment is heightened, and the task seems almost effortless. This "high" is achieved when the challenge just matches the person's skills; if it's too easy the experience is boring, too hard and it's frustrating. As people master tasks, they must seek greater challenges and match them with higher-level skills in order to keep experiencing flow. Csikszentmihalyi has argued that this is exactly what many people in creative pursuits do, a process that parallels the deliberate practice routine of continually pushing past one's current abilities.

The concept of flow might even help explain one of the particular puzzles of motivation to practice. It's a considerable "might" because the research has not been done. But the theory of deliberate practice keeps running up against a minor real-world contradiction. In the theory, practice is "not inherently enjoyable." Since it requires constantly trying to do things one can't quite do, and thus failing repeatedly, that makes sense. But in the research, top-level performers, at least in sports, often report the opposite. In studies of wrestlers, skaters, soccer players, field hockey players, and martial artists, practice activities rated fairly high on a scale of enjoyableness. As the tennis champion Monica Seles told the *New York Times* in 1999, "I just love to practice and drill and that stuff."

These reports contrast sharply with the feelings of Ericsson's violinists, who rated practice a pretty miserable way to spend their time. It may well be that athletes enjoy practice because for them it's a social activity, while for violinists it isn't. But at a deeper level one has to suspect that practice is somehow meeting an inner need for anyone who can maintain it at an intense level for years. It seems plausible that the role of practice in producing the highly enjoyable flow state could be part of it.

It certainly seems plausible as well that something more profound could also be going on. In some fields, such as science and math, fascination with the available problems seems to drive excellent performers. Benjamin Bloom, in his study of top-ranked young performers in several fields, found this motivation in some of them from their early years: "For most of the mathematicians, the joy of discovering a new way of solving a problem was more important than a high test score, receiving a good grade, or getting the teacher's approval for their work." Many studies of scientists have reported a similar finding; they get excited by new problems and find rewards not just in the solution but also in the process of seeking solutions.

In business, motivation has been the subject of endless research studies, books, articles, and consulting assignments. The all-time number 2 best-selling reprint from the *Harvard Business Review* is a 1968 article on motivation (the number 1 best seller is about time management). But the great majority of the research has focused on what motivates employees generally, not on what drives the top performers. Studies on that small subset have uncovered a wide range of driving forces, practically all of which are intrinsic. They may include a need for achievement, a need for power over others, even a need to do good in the world. But the drivers are almost never extrinsic, which makes sense when we observe the most eminent executives and entrepreneurs; long after they've accumulated more money than they could ever use and more fame than anyone could hope for, they keep working and trying to get better. It all fits with the big-picture idea that intrinsic drive is by far the most powerful.

Yet that can't be the whole story. Intrinsic motivation may dominate the big picture, but everyone, even the greatest achievers, has responded to extrinsic forces at critical moments. When Watson and Crick were struggling to find the structure of DNA, they worked almost nonstop because they knew they were in a race with other research teams. Alexander Graham Bell worked similarly on the telephone, knowing he was in competition with Elisha Gray, whom he beat to the patent office by just hours. Such people are driven by much more than fascination or joy.

In extensive research on what drives creative achievement, Teresa Amabile of the Harvard Business School at first proposed a simple hypothesis: "The intrinsically motivated state is conducive to creativity, whereas the extrinsically motivated state is detrimental." It's easy to see why she considered extrinsic motivation bad news; many studies showed exactly that. In one of Amabile's own projects, for example, college women were asked to make paper collages. Half the subjects were told their collages would be judged by graduate art students; the others were told that researchers were studying their mood and had no interest in the collages themselves. When the collages were then evaluated by a panel of artists, those produced by the subjects who expected to be judged were significantly less creative. Other studies showed that virtually any external attempt to constrain or control the work results in less creativity. Just being watched is detrimental. Even being offered a reward for doing the work results in less creative output than being offered nothing.

All these results were replicated many times. But other studies, going in other directions, were finding something else. Extrinsic motivators were of many types, not all of them controlling, and some of them seemed to enhance creativity. Specifically, extrinsic motivators that reinforce intrinsic motivation could work quite effectively. Like what? Recognition that confirms competence turned out to be effective. While the mere expectation of being judged tended to reduce creativity, personal feedback could actually enhance creativity if it was the right kind—"constructive, nonthreatening, and work-focused rather than person-focused," in Amabile's words. That is, feedback that helped a person do what he or she felt compelled to do was effective. Even the prospect of direct rewards, normally suffocating to creativity, could be helpful if they were the right kinds of rewards—those "that involve more time, freedom, or resources to pursue exciting ideas." These findings prompted Amabile to revise her hypothesis: Intrinsic motivation is still best, and extrinsic motivation that's controlling is still detrimental to creativity, but extrinsic motivators that reinforce intrinsic drives can be highly effective.

We've looked closely at motivation in creativity because, as noted, it has much to teach about the larger issue of what makes people persist through the demands of high achievement. Looking more broadly reveals further evidence that extrinsic motivators can, in certain circumstances, be helpful. For example, large parts of what we call creative work aren't very creative. Once a problem has been identified and solved—the creative part—it's necessary to evaluate the solution, write accounts of what was done, and communicate with others about it. All those jobs can be hard slogging, and the types of extrinsic motivators described above can be helpful in moving the work along.

More fundamentally, learning the skills of a particular field, one of the main objectives of deliberate practice, sometimes benefits from extrinsic motivators, especially in the early stages. Even the elite performers studied by Bloom required plenty of extrinsic motivation when they were starting out in their field. Their parents made them practice, as parents have always done, though it's interesting to note that in these cases, when push came to shove and parents had to make a direct threat, it frequently played off the student's intrinsic motivators. So it wasn't "If you don't do your piano practice we'll cancel your allowance," but rather "we'll sell the piano." Not "If you don't go to swimming practice you'll be grounded Saturday night," but rather "we'll take you off the team." If the child truly didn't care about the piano or swimming, the threats wouldn't have worked.

Other extrinsic motivators were also important, and while their effect was to help kids persevere through the challenges of deliberate practice, they were entirely consistent with the effective extrinsic motivators specified by Amabile for creativity. Feedback from coaches and teachers focused on the task and doing it better. Several teachers kept track of the child's performance, giving evidence to the child that he or she was making progress and could keep making progress. Recitals and contests were motivating because winning or doing well resulted in praise. Attention and acclaim, as a result of performing well, were significant motivators.

With time, however, "the students increasingly became responsible for their own motivation," Bloom reports. They set their own goals. Extrinsic motivators still played a role; students wanted to do well in public performances or competitions. But in part that was because doing so confirmed that they were making progress toward their goals, which is what they really cared about. These events also brought the students together with other top-level performers, so each student could figure out "what he or she must still do to reach the highest level of attainment possible." That is, the motivation wasn't just acclaim for performing well, but, increasingly, the inner drive to be the best.

How Organizations Blow It

It must be noted that, on this subject, as with the other findings on great performance, most organizations seem to be managed brilliantly for preventing people from performing at high levels. Since intrinsic drives are strongest, people will work most passionately and effectively on projects they choose for themselves. How many companies allow that? A few do, as noted in the previous chapter, and those companies have produced outstanding results. Yet most other companies steadfastly refuse to learn from them. Executives may protest that they have a business to manage and can't let employees run around working on who-knows-what. Fine; but those executives mustn't complain when their company's ideas are no better than the competition's. Nor should they claim to be mystified when employees lack passion and engagement.

How often is feedback at most companies constructive, nonthreatening, and work-focused rather than person-focused? Evaluations at most companies are exactly the opposite: telling the hapless employee what he did wrong, not how to do better, and specifying personal traits (attitude, personality) that must be changed, all under the unspoken looming threat of getting fired. This is so precisely unlike the way effective teachers and coaches help students persist in the demanding work of getting better that one can only gaze in wonder. A more potent system for discouraging people from the rigors of day-to-day improvement would be hard to design. As for rewards, at most companies they almost always entail more responsibilities and less freedom. Extra responsibilities are always part of rising higher in an organization, but if they don't come with the potential for more self-direction, the promotion will feel more like a burden than a reward. Extrinsic motivators may be, by definition, the only type that a company can offer employees, but most companies do it about as poorly as they can.

The weight of the evidence is that the drive to persist in the difficult job of improving, especially in adults, comes mostly from inside. Next question: How does it arise—that is, where does the passion come from? What determines who has it and who doesn't? Some researchers have argued that at least in some cases it's truly innate, present at birth. Ellen Winner, a professor of psychology at Boston College, years ago coined the wonderful term "the rage to master" to describe the overwhelming drive felt by some children, starting at extremely early ages, to work in a particular field. She has described, for example, the case of Peter, who started drawing at the age of ten months (versus two years for the average child) and before long "was waking up in the mornings and bellowing for paper and markers before getting out of bed." He drew obsessively virtually all day every day for years thereafter, and his drawings were very advanced, far beyond what the average child of his age could produce.

There are precocious children like Peter in many fields in addition to art, including music, chess, and math, and their stories are quite amazing. While most children have to be made to practice, these children can scarcely be restrained from it, and their performance is far beyond their years. What do these very powerful stories tell us?

One possible explanation is that these kids are somehow born with a compulsion to work in a particular domain. In keeping with the principles of great performance, they become very accomplished because they're practicing for huge numbers of hours. This explanation does not depend on any miracles, nor does it violate the ten-year rule; while these kids perform far in advance of other kids their age, they're still nowhere near world-class levels of achievement. That would have to wait much longer. In this theory, exactly why they were born with their specific compulsion remains a mystery. So far in the decoding of the human genome, no one has found a gene that compels a person to draw compulsively, or play the guitar or read or play chess, to name a few other fields in which precocity has turned up.

A different explanation, favored by Winner and some other researchers, is the reverse: Instead of compulsive practice producing high ability, high ability leads to compulsive practice. In this explanation, these kids are born not with a compulsion to practice but with an ability to learn far more quickly than average in a particular domain. They practice all the time, setting new goals for themselves and increasing their skill, because their ability to learn makes it so rewarding for them. This explanation would not seem to cover all cases; it seems extremely unlikely, for example, that Peter was drawing compulsively at ten months because of the progress he was making.

Note that this explanation is not merely a separate proposal for how the mechanism of deliberate practice gets set in motion. Winner argues that these precocious children are not just more diligent but also qualitatively different from others. Besides their higher ability to learn in their field, they also, in the case of artists, are more likely than average to be left-handed or ambidextrous and to be weak at verbal skills. In this theory, as in the previous one, exactly where the innate factor comes from—in this case, how a child is born with a superability to learn in a specific field—remains a mystery.

If neither of these explanations seems totally satisfying, they become even less so when we take a step back and consider the possibility that maybe the focus isn't quite right in either case. The drive we're looking for seems to be largely intrinsic, and that fact leads us to wonder what traits great performers are born with. But maybe that isn't as important as most of us assume it is. Intrinsic doesn't necessarily mean innate, that is, inborn. The idea that many of our traits and behaviors develop over time as a result of our experiences is noncontroversial, and everyone's life is an example. Possibly the intrinsic drive we're seeking also develops over time. It's tempting to focus on child prodigies because they clearly possess some kind of drive from such an early age that it seems it must be innate. Perhaps in some of those cases it is, though in some of them it may not be. Winner cites the case of Yani, a Chinese girl who by age five was producing paintings in the Chinese tradition that were strikingly skillful. Yani's father was an artist, and Winner reports that the young girl "spent many hours a day in her father's art studio painting alongside her father." Yani was a prodigy for sure, but from available evidence it would be hard to conclude that she was driven by anything truly inborn, either a compulsion to practice or an ability to learn, as distinct from the effects of spending all those hours with her artist father.

Even in those cases of child prodigies with proclivities that appear to be innate, studying them doesn't get us very far in understanding the passion behind great performance. That's because the large majority of these prodigies, as far as we can tell, don't grow up to be great performers. A few do, but most don't maintain the intensely focused daily work for the many years necessary to achieve at the highest levels. Whatever it is they bring into this world, it seems to be a star that shines brilliantly for a time and then usually fades. Josh Waitzkin, the child prodigy chess player whose story was told in the movie *Searching for Bobby Fischer,* suggested an explanation when he once told *Psychology Today,* "The most gifted kids in chess fall apart. They are told that they are winners, and when they inevitably run into a wall, they get stuck and think they must be losers."

Conversely, the people who do become top-level achievers are rarely child prodigies. That is certainly true in business; the early lives of the Welches, Ogilvies, and Rockefellers almost never hint at the success to come. Looking at more scientific research, this is one of the most notable findings in Bloom's large study, which examined performers at the highest level—people who had achieved national or international recognition before age forty. For example, all of the twenty-four pianists studied—each a finalist in at least one major international competition, such as the Van Cliburn or the Levintritt—had had lessons "forced upon them," in the words of the study, just the opposite of the kids who seemed driven to sit at the piano as toddlers. Similarly, in no case did the parents of the future champion swimmers foresee their child's eventual achievements. Time and again the story is the same: Even by age eleven or twelve it would have been difficult to predict who the future exceptional performers would be.

Even more important for our purposes, another common theme is that at some point not long past that age, these future achievers experienced an almost palpable shift in their stance toward their field. Their drive *became* intrinsic. One of the pianists recalled the life-changing experience at age fifteen of sitting just three feet away as a great pianist performed: "I remember feeling inundated and overwhelmed with the dynamic range, with the expressive potential, with hearing the real bite of the sound, the real softness of the sound. . . . at that point I became serious like I never had before. I cut out horsing around at the piano. I cut out sightreading for two hours a day just for the pleasure of it. I worked." Like all the pianists in the study, he had been forced to take lessons. It seems safe to say he had not been born with any kind of innate drive or rapid learning ability. But at that point he developed the intrinsic drive that would keep him going.

The Multiplier Effect

In our search for the source of the motivation that sustains people through the trials of getting better, the evidence is pushing in a clear direction. The passion doesn't accompany us into this world, but rather, like high-level skills themselves, it develops. That finding fits well with what we observe in real life. World-class achievers are driven to improve, but most of them didn't start out that way. We've already seen that in domains where it's possible to start work at an early age, such as music and sports, most future great performers need to be pushed at first. In domains where building the knowledge foundation takes many years before specific domain-related work can begin, such as business and high-level science, we commonly see that future stars may be decidedly undriven even as young adults. That was obviously the case with Steven Ballmer and Jeffrey Immelt sitting in their cubicle at Procter & Gamble. Both young men went on to business school (Ballmer to Stanford, Immelt to Harvard) and over time developed the drive to work prodigiously hard, not just in general, but specifically at building the particular skills that brought them to the top of the corporate world. Both men became famously focused workers. But they obviously did not possess that drive from day one.

If the drive to excel develops, rather than appearing fully formed, then how does it develop? Several researchers have separately proposed a mechanism that suggests an answer. Part of its appeal is that it helps explain why some people but not others develop high-level skills and at the same time develop the increasing motivation needed to do ever more advanced work. Stephen J. Ceci, Susan M. Barnett, and Tomoe Kanaya of Cornell University have called it the multiplier effect.

The concept is simple. A very small advantage in some field can spark a series of events that produce far larger advantages. For example, they say, imagine someone who is just slightly above average in

> eye-hand coordination, forearm strength, and reflexes. Initially, this individual may take satisfaction in doing slightly better at baseball than his schoolyard peers. . . . This satisfaction may lead such an individual to practice more, search more aggressively for others willing to play after school and on weekends, try out for teams (not just school teams but also summer league teams), get professional coaching, watch and discuss televised games, and so forth. Such an individual is likely to become matched with increasingly enriched environments for baseball skills. . . . Factors cascade over time because they multiply the effects of earlier, seemingly weak, factors.

It's easy to imagine the same process playing out in any other domain. As these researchers describe the general effect, "Each increase in competence is matched to a better environment, and, in turn, the better environment will be expected to further enhance their competence."

Note that this multiplier effect accounts not just for improvement of skills over time but also for the motivation that drives the improvement, as the young baseball player's satisfaction leads him to practice more. The sequence proposed by these researchers is strikingly similar to the actual experiences of future achievers reported in Bloom's research. He observed, "In all the fields most of these young students were regarded as fast learners by their first teachers. . . . Whether or not they were really faster learners than others is not known. . . . However, the attribution of 'fast learner' to them by the initial teacher was one major source of motivation. The teacher soon regarded and treated them as 'special' learners, and the students came to prize this very much."

Before long, the multiplier effect was clearly developing the drive of these students: "As they began to receive recognition for the talent in the early years of instruction, the children's investment in the talent became greater. No longer was the prime motivation to please parents and teachers. It now became the individual's special field of interest."

The concept of the multiplier effect is embedded in the fundamental theory of deliberate practice. Part of the way it works, as first explained by Anders Ericsson and his colleagues, is that a beginner's skills are so modest that he or she can manage only a little bit of deliberate practice, since it's highly demanding. But that little bit of practice increases the person's skills, making it possible to do more practice, which increases the person's skill level more. Thus, "In our framework we expect that increased level of acquired skill and performance would increase the maximal level of deliberate practice that can be sustained." The theory fits the evidence reported by others. In virtually every field, beginners can't manage more than an hour of practice per day, and sometimes much less. But by the time they become top performers, they've built themselves up to handling four to five hours a day. It isn't quite right to say only that the practice caused the performance or that the performance helped support the practice. Over time, each contributed to the other.

The evidence for the multiplier effect is powerful, in addition to which it makes sense and explains quite a bit. It then raises a very large question: What triggers the effect? If it all begins with some small advantage—a little difference that somehow tips a balance and starts a self-fueling cycle of increasing motivation and performance—where does that difference originate?

Ceci and his colleagues, in first describing the effect, assumed the difference was genetic; the reason that kid had better than average eye-hand coordination and other traits that gave him a small advantage in baseball is that he was born with them. Obviously this possibility cannot be denied, especially with regard to body traits that are heavily influenced by genes. In addition, it's easy to imagine how intelligence and other traits with a genetic component might trigger a multiplier effect, even if the significance of the genetic component is in dispute. After all, a small advantage is all it takes. We saw in chapter 3 that intelligence and other general abilities play a much smaller role in top-level performance than most of us believe, but even if intelligence isn't the critical performance factor in many fields, a small intelligence advantage at an early age could still trigger a multiplier effect that would produce exceptional performance many years later. Clearly these traits would not be guaranteed to set off multiplier effects in every case. If the kid with the baseball advantage lived in a time or place where baseball was unheard of, he'd be out of luck, and we can easily imagine endless other scenarios in which some trait that could conceivably trigger a multiplier effect in one setting would produce no effect in another.

The much more intriguing possibility is that events or situations having nothing to do with innate traits could also set off multiplier effects. An example that seems to occur quite often is what happens when someone begins training at an earlier age than others in the field. Many researchers have observed that as people start learning skills in virtually any field, they're typically compared not against the world's greatest performers in that field but against others their own age. Nobody considered whether the ten-year-old Tiger Woods was a threat to the top professionals; what mattered was that he was much better than other ten-year-olds. One way to get a very good shot at performing better than others of the same age is to start training earlier than they do (as Woods did), thus accumulating more deliberate practice. Standing out at any given age is an excellent way to attract attention and praise, fueling the multiplier, and it can be done without relying on any innate ability. It's worth noting that studies of swimmers, gymnasts, chess players, violinists, and pianists show that the more accomplished performers started training at earlier ages.

A similar way to ignite the multiplier effect is to begin learning skills in a place where competition is sparse. It's a lot easier to stand out as a math whiz when your town has only a hundred other kids your age than when it has a hundred thousand. Many of the young achievers in Bloom's study reported the same experience: being local celebrities, only to move on to a higher level of competition and find that plenty of others are at least as good as they are. As one of the pianists recalled about his arrival at an elite music school, "It was a shock. It's not easy to find out that there are other people who really play very well when you've been isolated and made to think you're something." But it's okay; by this time, these performers had developed the drive to keep going. Would they have developed that drive in a setting where they received an early message that they were nothing special? Howard Gardner, in his study of Einstein, Stravinsky, and other exceptional creators, observed that they generally didn't come from major cities. Instead, they developed their skills in smaller environments and then moved on to the big time.

Could the multiplier effect even be triggered in what we might call the opposite way? It seems plausible that mildly superior performance at an early age or in a small milieu, no matter how attained, could attract the extra praise that builds motivation for more intense practice, and so on. But since the process is circular, could we start it spinning not with superior performance but with extra praise? That is, could simply telling someone that he or she is especially good, regardless of actual performance, motivate the extra practice that leads to improved performance, attracting more praise, and so on? This also seems plausible. Recall that, even though Bloom had no evidence that his research subjects were fast learners, their teachers saw them that way. He reported that, in general, "The teacher soon regarded and treated them as 'special' learners, and the students came to prize this very much." In addition, many of these students had parents who told them they were special, as parents so often do, regardless of actual evidence. Here again, it seems possible that a factor quite independent of any innate ability could start the multiplier effect turning, or at least give it a good shove.

It seems possible, and even likely based on available evidence—but it isn't proven. The rigorous research that would nail down this possibility hasn't been done. It could be and perhaps will be. Stephen Ceci and his colleagues believe "it is a testable empirical question" whether "environmental factors"—such things as earlier deliberate practice, extra praise, or others—could "jump start the dynamic multiplier effect." But they conclude that so far "this has not been tested in an empirically adequate manner." So we just don't know for sure.

What Do You Believe?

That conclusion is highly significant for our purposes because it means that, research-wise, we've reached the end of the line. It's the end of the line not just on the question of motivation, but also in a much larger sense.

Our quest for the source of great performance has taken us past many wrong turns and through a great deal of useful knowledge, and has led us finally to the issue of where the drive to persevere comes from. We've learned a lot even about that. Most significant, we've seen that the passion develops, rather than emerging suddenly and fully formed. We've also seen hints that childhood may be especially important in how the drive's development gets started. Anders Ericsson goes so far as to say, "The research frontier is parenting. Push children too hard and they respond with anger. You have to develop an independent individual who has chosen to be involved in this activity. It's how you as a parent can make individuals feel freed to reach these levels and aware that this is going to be a long process." Yes, maybe that is what it's all about. But as he says, that's the research frontier. The work hasn't been done yet.

Ultimately, we cannot get to the very heart of this matter; we cannot explain fully and generally why certain people put themselves through the years or decades of punishing, intensive daily work that eventually makes them world-class great. We've reached the point where we are left without guidance from the scientists and must proceed by looking in the only place we have left, which is within ourselves.

What would cause you to do the enormous work necessary to be a top-performing CEO, Wall Street trader, jazz pianist, courtroom lawyer, or anything else? Would anything? The answers depend on your answers to two basic questions: What do you really want? And what do you really believe?

What you want—really, deeply want—is fundamental because deliberate practice is a heavy investment. Becoming a great performer demands the largest investment you will ever make—many years of your life devoted utterly to your goal—and only someone who wants to reach that goal with extraordinary power can make it. We often see the price people pay in their rise to the top of any field; even if their marriages or other relationships survive, their interests outside their field typically cannot. Howard Gardner, after studying his seven exceptional achievers, noted that "usually, as a means of being able to continue work, the creator sacrificed normal relationships in the personal sphere." Such people are "committed obsessively to their work. Social life or hobbies are almost immaterial." That may sound like admirable self-sacrifice and direction of purpose, but it often goes much further, and it can be ugly. As Gardner notes, "the self-confidence merges with egotism, egocentrism, and narcissism: each of the creators seems highly self-absorbed, not only wholly involved in his or her own projects, but likely to pursue them at the cost of other individuals." The story of the great achiever who leaves a wake of anger and betrayal is a common one.

So what would it take for you to accept all of that in pursuit of a goal? What would you want so much that you'd commit yourself to the necessary hard, endless work, giving up relationships and other interests, so that you might eventually get it? Whatever it is that the greatest performers want, that's how much they must want it.

The second question is more profound. What do you really believe? Do you believe that you have a choice in this matter? Do you believe that if you do the work, properly designed, with intense focus for hours a day and years on end, your performance will grow dramatically better and eventually reach the highest levels? If you believe that, then there's at least a chance you will do the work and achieve great performance.

But if you believe that your performance is forever limited by your lack of a specific innate gift, or by a lack of general abilities at a level that you think must be necessary, then there's no chance at all that you will do the work.

That's why this belief is tragically constraining. Everyone who has achieved exceptional performance has encountered terrible difficulties along the way. There are no exceptions. If you believe that doing the right kind of work can overcome the problems, then you have at least a chance of moving on to ever better performance. But those who see the setbacks as evidence that they lack the necessary gift will give up—quite logically, in light of their beliefs. They will never achieve what they might have.

What you really believe about the source of great performance thus becomes the foundation of all you will ever achieve. As we noted much earlier, such beliefs can be extremely deep-seated. Regardless of where our beliefs in this matter originated, however, we all have the opportunity to base them on the evidence of reality.

The evidence offers no easy assurances. It shows that the price of top-level achievement is extraordinarily high. Perhaps it's inevitable that not many people will choose to pay it. But the evidence shows also that by understanding how a few become great, anyone can become better. Above all, what the evidence shouts most loudly is striking, liberating news: that great performance is not reserved for a preordained few. It is available to you and to everyone.

Acknowledgments

This book would not have been written if my *Fortune* colleague Jerry Useem hadn't walked into my office and asked if I wanted to write something for a special issue on great performance in business. It turned out I'd been waiting a long time for that question. I held strong views and had considerable curiosity about the topic, far more than I realized.

The resulting article provoked a more intense response than anything else I've written. It was certainly e-mailed a lot, but beyond that, it seemed to reach readers in a deeper way. Several people told me they had read it aloud to their kids, which is not a reaction we often get to an article in a business magazine. People thanked me for writing it, even many months after it appeared. I suspected there was more to be said.

So thank you, Jerry, and thank you to Hank Gilman, Eric Pooley, and the other *Fortune* editors who helped bring the article to publication.

Professor K. Anders Ericsson, Conradi Eminent Scholar at Florida State University, whom we met several times in this book, was extremely generous with his time and thoughts. As I hope is clear, his work over the past thirty years, on his own and with colleagues, formed the foundation of many of the ideas presented here. He deserves special thanks because this book could not have been written without him.

Adrian Zackheim, Adrienne Schultz, and the team at Penguin Group (USA) were encouraging and supportive at every turn, which makes a difference to an author.

Bob Barnett and Dineen Howell of Williams & Connolly represented me superbly, as always.

Most of all I must thank my family for their understanding and support during a project that I should have known would be more work than I thought.

Sources

Chapter One: The Mystery

For research on how some types of auditor skills diminish over time, see Jean Bedard, Michelene T. H. Chi, Lynford E. Graham, and James Shanteau, "Expertise in Auditing," *Auditing 12* (suppl., 1993), pp. 1–25.

An excellent summary of the research showing how experience does not necessarily lead to outstanding performance—including the research on clinical psychologists, surgeons, and others cited in this chapter—is found in Colin F. Camerer and Eric J. Johnson, "The Process-Performance Paradox in Expert Judgment: How Can Experts Know So Much and Predict So Badly?" in K. Anders Ericsson and Jacqui Smith, eds., *Toward a General Theory of Expertise: Prospects and Limits* (New York: Cambridge University Press, 1991), pp. 195–217.

The description of "the experience trap" is in Kishore Sengupta, Tarek K. Abdel-Hamid, and Luk N. Van Wassenhove, "The Experience Trap," *Harvard Business Review,* February 2008, pp. 94–101.

Physicians' scores on tests of medical knowledge declining with experience: N. K. Choudhry, R. H. Fletcher, and S. B. Soumerai, "Systematic Review: The Relationship Between Clinical Experience and Quality of Health Care," *Annals of Internal Medicine 142* (2005), pp. 260–73.

Physicians' declining skill at diagnosing heart sounds and X-rays: K. A. Ericsson, "Deliberate Practice and the Acquisition of Expert Performance in Medicine and Related Domains," *Academic Medicine 10* (2004), S70–S81.

The work of Dr. Niels H. Secher of the University of Copenhagen is reported in Gina Kolata, "Bigger Is Better, Except When It's Not," *The New York Times,* September 27, 2007, p. G1.

The study that demonstrates rising standards in chess over the past two

centuries is Roy W. Roring and K. A. Ericsson (in preparation), "The Measurement of the Highest Levels of Productive Thought: An Application to
World Championship Performance in Chess."

Data on the amounts of shareholder wealth created by Microsoft,
Procter & Gamble, and other companies comes from the firm EVA Dimen-
sions, which calculates these figures for most of the companies in the
Russell 3000. Figures cited in this chapter are for February 5, 2008.

Data on Exxon Mobil's use of cash comes from 2006 financial statements. The quotation from CEO Rex Tillerson is from a personal interview
conducted on March 1, 2007.

The quotation attributed to Josh Billings has been attributed also to
Mark Twain, Artemus Ward, and other nineteenth-century American writers. Billings looks like the best bet to me, but if anyone has definitive evidence I'd love to know about it.

Chapter Two: Talent Is Overrated

The study of musical achievement in English students is John A. Sloboda,
Jane W. Davidson, Michael J. A. Howe, and Derek G. Moore, "The Role of
Practice in the Development of Performing Musicians," *British Journal of
Psychology 87* (1996), pp. 287–309.

The importance of Francis Galton is apparent from the fact that his
major works are still in print. Quotations cited in this chapter come
from the following edition: Francis Galton, *Hereditary Genius: An Inquiry
into its Laws and Consequences* (Amherst, N.Y.: Prometheus Books,
1869/2006).

The study of outstanding pianists referred to briefly is part of a landmark
work that we will examine more closely later: Benjamin S. Bloom, ed.,
Developing Talent in Young People (New York: Ballantine Books, 1985).

The analysis of Mozart's development is based largely on the work
of Professor Robert W. Weisberg of Temple University. Two of his written works were especially helpful: Robert W. Weisberg, "Creativity
and Knowledge: A Challenge to Theories," in Robert J. Sternberg, ed.,
Handbook of Creativity (New York: Cambridge University Press, 1999), and
Robert W. Weisberg, *Creativity: Beyond the Myth of Genius* (New York:
W. H. Freeman & Co., 1993).

The precocity index used to compare the technical virtuosity of musical performers is described in: A. C. Lehmann and K. A. Ericsson, "The Historical Development of Domains of Expertise: Performance Standards and Innovations in Music," in A. Steptoe, ed., *Genius and the Mind* (Oxford: Oxford University Press, 1998), pp. 67–94.

Neal Zaslaw's very entertaining and erudite paper is Neal Zaslaw, "Mozart as a Working Stiff," in James M. Morris, ed., *On Mozart* (New York: Cambridge University Press, 1994).

The Alex Ross quotation is from Alex Ross, "The Storm of Style," *The New Yorker,* July 24, 2006.

Earl Woods's account of how he managed Tiger's development as a golfer is Earl Woods with Pete McDaniel, *Training a Tiger: A Father's Guide to Raising a Winner in Both Golf and Life* (New York: HarperCollins, 1997).

Also helpful in providing useful information on Tiger's development was Lawrence J. Londino, *Tiger Woods: A Biography* (Westport, Conn.: Greenwood Press, 2006).

Jack Welch's story comes from knowing him for many years and from his first book: Jack Welch with John A. Byrne, *Jack: Straight from the Gut* (New York: Warner Business Books, 2001).

The stories of Bill Gates, John D. Rockefeller, and David Ogilvy come largely from the following works: Bill Gates, *The Road Ahead* (New York: Viking Penguin, 1995); Ron Chernow, *Titan: The Life of John D. Rockefeller, Sr.* (New York: Random House, 1998); and David Ogilvy, *Confessions of an Advertising Man* (New York: Atheneum, 1963).

The story of Warren Buffett comes from having interviewed him formally and informally many times, as well as from the many articles about him by the great Carol Loomis of *Fortune.* One article remains especially insightful: Carol J. Loomis, "The Inside Story of Warren Buffett," *Fortune,* April 11, 1988.

Chapter Three: How Smart Do You Have to Be?

The academic paper first describing the experiment involving the undergraduate SF is K. A. Ericsson, W. G. Chase, and S. Faloon, "Acquisition of Memory Skill," *Science 208* (1980), 1181–82. The research has been described at greater length in a number of other papers. In addition, I spoke with Professor Ericsson about the experiment, and he provided an audio tape of the session on July 11, 1978, which I describe in this chapter.

Professor James R. Flynn is an extremely thoughtful researcher on intelligence. See James R. Flynn, *What Is Intelligence?* (New York: Cambridge University Press, 2007).

The study of salespeople is Andrew J. Vinchur, Jeffrey S. Schippmann, Fred S. Switzer III, and Philip L. Roth, "A Meta-analytic Review of Predictors of Job Performance for Salespeople," *Journal of Applied Psychology, 83*, no. 4 (1998), pp. 586–97.

The study of racetrack patrons is Stephen J. Ceci, and Jeffrey K. Liker, "A Day at the Races: A Study of IQ, Expertise, and Cognitive Complexity," *Journal of Experimental Psychology: General* 115, no. 3 (1986), pp. 255–66.

The finding that some chess players at the international master level possess below-average IQs is one of the most surprising and intriguing in this field. It is in J. Doll and U. Mayr, "Intelligence and Achievement in Chess—A Study of Chess Masters," *Psychologische Beiträge 29* (1987), pp. 270–89.

The research on chess players and how well they can recall the positions of pieces on the board has proven to be extremely important in the study of great performance because it reveals that the seemingly incredible memories of chess experts are developed and specific to chess, not innate and general. Three researchers built the foundation of this work. One was a Dutch researcher, A. D. de Groot, whose doctoral dissertation was written in 1946 but not translated into English until 1965. The other two are William Chase and Herbert Simon, whose research showed that chess experts could remember the positions of many pieces in actual chess positions but were scarcely better than novices at remembering the positions of pieces placed randomly. See A. D. de Groot, *Thought and Choice in Chess* (The Hague: Mouton, 1946/1965); W. G. Chase and H. A. Simon, "Perception in Chess," *Cognitive Psychology 4* (1973), pp. 55–81; and W. G. Chase and H. A. Simon, "The Mind's Eye in Chess," in W. G. Chase, ed., *Visual Information Processing* (New York: Academic Press, 1973), pp. 215–81.

The story of Robert Rubin comes from a personal interview with him on March 23, 2007, and from his book: Robert Rubin and Jacob Weisberg, *In an Uncertain World* (New York: Random House, 2003).

Chapter Four: A Better Idea

The basic facts of Jerry Rice's biography are very widely available in any number of published accounts. The specifics of his records are from www.nfl.com.

The study of violinists at the Music Academy of West Berlin is part of a highly influential paper that has become the foundation of the deliberate practice framework: K. Anders Ericsson, Ralf Th. Krampe, and Clemens Tesch-Römer, "The Role of Deliberate Practice in the Acquisition of Expert Performance," *Psychological Review 100*, no. 3 (1993), pp. 363–406.

Chapter Five: What Deliberate Practice Is and Isn't

The specific elements of deliberate practice are all to be found in the description presented in the foundational paper cited above, though these elements are not discussed individually at length. The elements are considered more deeply in a number of later papers; a good introduction, with references to other research, is K. Anders Ericsson, "The Acquisition of Expert Performance: An Introduction to Some of the Issues," in K. Anders Ericsson, ed., *The Road to Excellence: The Acquisition of Expert Performance in the Arts and Sciences, Sports and Games* (Mahwah, N.J.: Lawrence Erlbaum Associates, 1996).

The account of Moe Norman is from a chapter in the book cited above: Janet L. Starkes, Janice M. Deakin, Fran Allard, Nicola J. Hodges, and April Hayes, "Deliberate Practice in Sports: What Is It Anyway?"

The account of Chris Rock's preparation for his New Year's Eve performance at Madison Square Garden, illustrating all the elements of deliberate practice, is David Carr, "Hard at Work on New Year's Eve," *The New York Times*, December 28, 2007.

The account of the Polgar sisters is taken primarily from Carlin Flora, "The Grandmaster Experiment," *Psychology Today*, July/August 2005; and "Queen Takes All," *The Telegraph*, January 16, 2002.

The description of how professional singers experience a singing lesson very differently from the way amateurs do is from C. Grape, M. Sandgren,

L. O. Hansson, M. Ericson, and T. Theorell, "Does Singing Promote Well-being? An Empirical Study of Professional and Amateur Singers During a Singing Lesson," *Integrative Physiological and Behavioral Science 38* (2003), pp. 65–71.

For a particularly passionate explication of the case against a strict nature-versus-nurture separation in understanding development, see David S. Moore, *The Dependent Gene: The Fallacy of "Nature vs. Nurture"* (New York: Owl Books, 2001).

Until the expert performance research of the past thirty years, the prevailing view among psychologists was that performance at its highest level was largely automatic. The standard description is in P. Fitts and M. I. Posner, *Human Performance* (Belmont, Calif.: Brooks/Cole, 1967).

The opposite view, that top performers reach their high levels of achievement in part by avoiding automaticity, is described in K. Anders Ericsson, "The Influence of Experience and Deliberate Practice on the Development of Superior Expert Performance," in K. Anders Ericsson, Neil Charness, Paul J. Feltovich, and Robert R. Hoffman, eds., *The Cambridge Handbook of Expertise and Expert Performance* (New York: Cambridge University Press, 2006).

Chapter Six: How Deliberate Practice Works

The original work on how an expert tennis player predicts the flight of his opponent's serve based on cues in his posture is C. M. Jones and T. R. Miles, "Use of Advance Cues in Predicting the Flight of a Lawn Tennis Ball," *Journal of Human Movement Studies 4* (1978), pp. 231–35.

Similar findings have since been produced in several other sports. For a recent discussion of the general topic, see A. Mark Williams, Paul Ward, and Nicholas J. Smeeton, "Perceptual and Cognitive Expertise in Sport: Implications for Skill Acquisition and Performance Enhancement," in A. Mark Williams and Nicola J. Hodges, eds., *Skill Acquisition in Sport: Research, Theory, and Practice* (Abingdon, U.K.: Routledge, 2004).

The findings on expert typists' ability to look farther ahead in the text is in T. A. Salthous, "Effects of Age and Skill in Typing," *Journal of Experimental Psychology: General 113* (1984), pp. 345–71.

The findings on drivers and how they respond to hazardous situations, as well as research on pilots mentioned later in the chapter, are summarized in Francis T. Durso and Andrew R. Dattel, "Expertise and Transportation," in K. Anders Ericsson, Neil Charness, Paul J. Feltovich, and Robert R. Hoffman, eds., *The Cambridge Handbook of Expertise and Expert Performance* (New York: Cambridge University Press, 2006).

The research showing how expert jugglers need to see only the apex of the balls' trajectories is in P. J. Beek, *Juggling Dynamics* (Amsterdam: Free University Press, 1989).

The research on how expert radiologists read X-rays, as well as research on how physicists and psychological counselors categorize problems cited later in this chapter, is summarized in the following chapter in the *Cambridge Handbook:* Michelene T. H. Chi, "Laboratory Methods for Assessing Experts' and Novices' Knowledge."

The overview of the role of knowledge in expert systems, quoted in this chapter, is also from the *Cambridge Handbook.* The chapter is Bruce G. Buchanan, Randall Davis, and Edward A. Feigenbaum, "Expert Systems: A Perspective from Computer Science."

The quotations of Jeffrey Immelt are from "Growth as a Process: The HBR Interview," *Harvard Business Review,* June 2006.

The paper proposing the theoretical framework of long-term working memory is K. Anders Ericsson and Walter Kintsch, "Long-Term Working Memory," *Psychological Review 102,* no. 2 (1995), pp. 211–45.

The research on memory for key events in a written description of a baseball game is in H. L. Chiesi, G. J. Spilich, and J. F. Voss, "Acquisition of Domain-Related Information in Relation to High and Low Domain Knowledge," *Journal of Verbal Learning and Verbal Behavior 18* (1979), pp. 257–74.

An overview of the evidence showing how the body changes in response to years of deliberate practice, along with references to many supporting articles, can be found in Ericsson's article on experience and deliberate practice in the *Cambridge Handbook.* The findings on brain changes are summarized in the following chapter from the *Cambridge Handbook:* Nicole M. Hill and Walter Schneider, "Brain Changes in the Development of Expertise: Neuroanatomical and Neurophysiological Evidence About Skill-Based Adaptations."

Chapter Seven: Applying the Principles in Our Lives

Benjamin Franklin's autobiography, being long past copyright protection, is easily available online.

The research on self-regulation, which is the basis for the guidelines on performing deliberate practice as a part of work, is summarized in the following chapter of the *Cambridge Handbook:* Barry J. Zimmerman, "Development and Adaptation of Expertise: The Role of Self-Regulatory Processes and Beliefs."

The reference to Professor Michael Porter of the Harvard Business School and his ability to educate himself on a given company through twenty hours of library research is from a highly memorable personal conversation almost thirty years ago.

The research on how expert and novice firefighters perceive fires differently is in G. A. Klein, *Sources of Power: How People Make Decisions* (Cambridge, Mass.: MIT Press, 1998).

Chapter Eight: Applying the Principles in Our Organizations

The reference to Judy Pahren of Capital One Financial and the quotations of Jeffrey Immelt, Kenneth Chenault, Noel Tichy, Colonel Thomas Kolditz, David Nadler, John McConnell, Ram Charan, and Colonel Stas Preczewski are from personal interviews.

Much of this chapter is based on research conducted by Hewitt Associates for its 2007 Top Companies for Leaders project. This research involved more than five hundred companies around the world. Hewitt collected extensive information from each one, conducted interviews with executives, and performed financial analyses. The resulting voluminous data, including interview transcripts, were made available to me as *Fortune* magazine's representative. *Fortune* published an extensive summary of the findings, as well as an accompanying article by me, in the edition of October 1, 2007.

The material on teams and the many ways they go wrong is based on an article I wrote for *Fortune* titled "Why Dream Teams Fail" in the edition of June 12, 2006.

Chapter Nine: Performing Great at Innovation

The quotation of Adrian Slywotzky is from a personal interview.

Much of the evidence presented in this chapter is summarized in Professor Robert W. Weisberg's paper, "Creativity and Knowledge: A Challenge to Theories," cited in the notes for chapter 2.

The research by Dean Keith Simonton, showing that the relation between education and creative eminence looks like an inverted *U,* is in D. K. Simonton, *Genius, Creativity, and Leadership* (New York: Cambridge University Press, 1984).

The famous experiments of the Luchinses, involving jars of varying capacities, are described in A. S. Luchins and E. H. Luchins, *Rigidity of Behavior* (Eugene, Ore.: University of Oregon Press, 1959).

The research by Professor John R. Hayes on composers, painters, and poets is in J. R. Hayes, "Cognitive Processes in Creativity," in J. A. Glover, R. R. Bonning, and C. R. Reynolds, eds., *Handbook of Creativity* (New York: Plenum, 1989).

Professor Howard Gardner's fascinating study of seven famous creators is Howard Gardner, *Creating Minds* (New York: Basic Books, 1993).

Professor Weisberg's detailed descriptions of how Watson and Crick found the structure of DNA, and of Watt's work on the steam engine and Whitney's work on the cotton gin, is in his book, *Creativity: Beyond the Myth of Genius,* cited in the notes for chapter 2. This is also where he discusses the possible origins of Coleridge's *Kubla Khan.*

The *New York Times* article on the development of the FLY computer pen and related matter is Janet Rae-Dupree, "Eureka! It Really Takes Years of Hard Work," *The New York Times,* February 3, 2008.

The comments on Big-C, little-c, and mini-c creativity are in Ronald A. Beghetto and James C. Kaufman, "The Genesis of Creative Greatness: mini-c and the Expert Performance Approach," in *High Ability Studies 18,* no. 1 (2007), pp. 59–61.

The McKinsey study on innovation is Joanna Barsh, Marla M. Capozzi, and Jonathan Davidson, "Leadership and Innovation," *The McKinsey Quarterly*, no. 1 (2008), pp. 37–47.

The quotation of Professor Raymond S. Nickerson is from Raymond S. Nickerson, "Enhancing Creativity," in Robert J. Sternberg, ed., *Handbook of Creativity* (New York: Cambridge University Press, 1999).

The quotation of David N. Perkins is from David N. Perkins, "The Nature and Nurture of Creativity," in B. F. Jones and L. Idol, eds., *Dimensions of Thinking and Cognitive Instruction* (Hillsdale, N.J.: Erlbaum, 1990).

Chapter Ten: Great Performance in Youth and Age

The paper on Nobel Prize winners and other innovators, and why they're getting older, is Benjamin F. Jones, "Age and Great Invention," NBER Working Paper no. 11359 (2005).

Dean Keith Simonton's comments about the importance of the supporting environment are in his paper in the *Cambridge Handbook,* entitled "Historiometric Methods."

Benjamin Bloom's important study of creative development in young people was cited in the notes for chapter 2.

The research showing the importance of home environments that are both structured and stimulating is described in M. Csikszentmihalyi, K. Rathunde, and S. Whalen, *Talented Teenagers: The Roots of Success and Failure* (New York: Cambridge University Press, 1993).

Much of the research of aging cited here, including the research showing that pianists suffer normal age-related declines except in piano-related skills, is summarized in a chapter of the *Cambridge Handbook:* Ralf Th. Krampe and Neil Charness, "Aging and Expertise."

The account of Julio Franco's training regimen is in Ben Shpigel, "Breakfast at Julio's," *The New York Times,* March 1, 2006, p. D1.

The quotation of Karl Malone is from an excellent general article on aging athletes: Martin Miller, "Raising the Bar at 40," *The Los Angeles Times,* September 29, 2003.

Chapter Eleven: Where Does the Passion Come From?

The study that found that elite figure skaters spent more time working on jumps they couldn't do is Janice M. Deakin and Stephen Cobley, "A Search for Deliberate Practice: An Examination of the Practice Environments in Figure Skating and Volleyball," in Janet L. Starkes and K. Anders Ericsson, eds., *Expert Performance in Sports: Advances in Research on Sports Expertise* (Champaign, Ill.: Human Kinetics, 2003).

Csikszentmihalyi's observations suggesting a possible source of intrinsic motivation that seems to mesh well with the characteristics of deliberate practice are in his acclaimed book: M. Csikszentmihalyi, *Flow: The Psychology of Optimal Experience* (New York: Harper & Row, 1990).

A good overview of Teresa Amabile's very extensive work on creativity and its motivation, with references to specific studies and articles, is in Mary Ann Collins and Teresa M. Amabile, "Motivation and Creativity," in Robert J. Sternberg, ed., *Handbook of Creativity* (New York: Cambridge University Press, 1999).

A summary of Winner's argument, with many fascinating examples, is in Ellen Winner, "The Rage to Master: The Decisive Role of Talent in the Visual Arts," in K. Anders Ericsson, ed., *The Road to Excellence: The Acquisition of Expert Performance in the Arts and Sciences, Sports and Games* (Mahwah, N.J.: Lawrence Erlbaum Associates, 1996).

The quotation of Josh Waitzkin about the sad fate of many of the most accomplished child chess players is from the *Psychology Today* article on the Polgar sisters cited above.

The quotation of Jeffrey Immelt, and the description of him and Steve Ballmer sitting side by side at Procter & Gamble as twenty-two-year-olds, is from a personal interview with Immelt.

The description of the multiplier effect is in Stephen J. Ceci, Susan M. Barnett, and Tomoe Kanaya, "Developing Childhood Proclivities into Adult Competencies: The Overlooked Multiplier Effect," in Robert J. Sternberg and Elena L. Grigorenko, eds., *The Psychology of Abilities, Competencies, and Expertise* (New York: Cambridge University Press, 2003).

The quotation of Anders Ericsson about parenting as the research frontier is from a personal interview.

Index